Get Outside!

Help Us Keep This Guide Up to Date

Every effort has been made by the authors and editors to make this guide as accurate and useful as possible. However, many things can change after a guide is published—trails are rerouted, regulations change, techniques evolve, facilities come under new management, e-mail addresses and Web sites change, etc.

We would love to hear from you concerning your experiences with this guide and how you feel it could be improved and kept up to date. While we may not be able to respond to all comments and suggestions, we'll take them to heart and we'll also make certain to share them with the author. Please send your comments and suggestions to the following address:

The Globe Pequot Press
Reader Response/Editorial Department
P.O. Box 480
Guilford, CT 06437

Or you may e-mail us at:

editorial@globe-pequot.com

Thanks for your input, and happy travels!

Get Outside!

**American
Hiking
Society**

FALCON®

Guilford, Connecticut
An imprint of The Globe Pequot Press

Falcon is a registered trademark of The Globe Pequot Press.

ISBN 0-7627-2380-7

Library of Congress Cataloging-in-Publication Data is available.

Manufactured in the United States of America
First Edition/First Printing

Contents

How to Use This Directory

Listings are arranged by state. Each entry includes a description of the area, types of volunteer opportunities available, position requirements, and volunteer benefits. Also listed is the contact person's information, including mailing address. Phone numbers and e-mail addresses are also included when provided by the agency or group.

Many agencies, because of budget restraints, cannot guarantee all the described benefits will be available. This is especially true of stipends and per diem or subsistence allowances. To avoid disappointments or misunderstandings, the volunteer should reach an agreement with the agencies before reporting to work.

Finding a volunteer job is easy if you follow a few simple guidelines:

Decide (state or region) where you want to work, what kind of work you'd like to do, and the type of lands in which you would be interested in working.

Skim through the listings to find openings that suit you.

When you have picked the positions you like best, write or call the contact person listed to make sure work is still available.

In your letter or during your call, ask questions that will prepare you for your trip: What kind of weather should you expect? What equipment should you bring? Will you be reimbursed for out-of-pocket expenses? Will you have to pay for food? How long will the assignment last?

Reach an understanding with your contact person. You may be asked to send a resume or fill out application forms.

When you are accepted, show up on the appointed day as agreed. The agency is counting on you.

Job Descriptions

CAMPGROUND HOSTS stay for extended periods in scenic campgrounds and meet people from all over the country and from foreign lands. Hosts must be cheerful, outgoing, and enjoy interacting with people.

These volunteers answer questions, help campers get settled, suggest things to do and see in the area, and explain campground rules and regulations. Hosts usually help keep the ground neat and clean and sometimes perform light maintenance work. Hosts may be asked to collect fees. In exchange for their work, most volunteers receive a free campsite for the length of the position. Hosts usually provide their own trailer, camper, or RV unit; be aware that not all campgrounds have water hookups. Be sure to fully understand what you will be asked to do—and what you will get in return—before reporting for duty.

TRAIL MAINTENANCE and TRAIL CREW volunteers work hard. They clear brush, grub out stumps, trim vegetation, remove downed trees, repair erosion damage, and basically keep trails open. The work is strenuous, so volunteers must be in good physical condition. Trail crews will use tools like shovels, picks, Pulaskis, saws, and, on occasion, chain saws. Sometimes workers will pack in equipment via pack animals.

WILDERNESS RANGERS and BACKCOUNTRY GUARDS spend summers in some of America's most beautiful country, hiking trails by day and camping out at night. Whether camping at a backcountry site or in a cabin, these workers are often alone for days at a time. It is an active, vigorous job, one that requires the ranger to hike 10 to 20 miles a day while carrying thirty- to fifty-pound loads.

Much of the work involves contact with visitors, informing them of wilderness regulations, zero-impact camping techniques, and safety considerations. The volunteer ranger will clear and maintain trails, clean-up backcountry campsites, and repair and replace signs.

Wilderness rangers must be comfortable approaching and interacting with strangers and must be in very good physical condition. The volunteer usually provides his or her own personal equipment.

CLUB WORK. Many of our member clubs and organizations are listed in this directory and provide a variety of volunteer opportunities. If you are interested in maintaining trails on weekend work trips, give them a call to see if your skills would be useful for any of their projects.

Get Outside! is published by The Globe Pequot Press and American Hiking Society, with financial support from the USDA Forest Service and the Bureau of Land Management. Every attempt has been made to make it as complete and accurate as possible. Inclusion does not imply confirmation of the information.

Nationwide

American Hiking Society

Agency: American Hiking Society
Season: Year-round
Contact: Alliance Coordinator
1422 Fenwick Lane
Silver Spring, MD 20910
E-mail: info@AmericanHiking.org
Web: www.AmericanHiking.org
Phone: (301) 565–6704

Description/Positions Available: The American Hiking Society's Alliance of Hiking Organizations is a network of more than 150 organizations working to maintain footpaths, conserve trail lands, and protect the hiking experience.

Many Alliance organizations are listed in this directory with their volunteer opportunities; many others are not. To locate a club in your area and offer your help, please visit our Web site or call the AHS Alliance department.

American Hiking Society, Volunteer Vacations

Agency: American Hiking Society
Season: Year-round
Contact: Shirley Hearn
1422 Fenwick Lane
Silver Spring, MD 20910
E-mail: volvac@AmericanHiking.org
Web: www.AmericanHiking.org
Phone: (800) 972–8608, extension 206

Description/Positions Available: The American Hiking Society sends crews each spring, summer, and fall to build and repair trails in national parks, forests, and rangelands. Each year, AHS will send more than 100 crews to locations including Alaska, Arizona, and Colorado. Armed with picks and shovels, crews will build and restore trails and assist with a variety of projects designed to make these areas safe, attractive and accessible. Volunteer Vacations crews consist of people eighteen and older who are in good physical condition and who want to combine an enjoyable vacation with hard work to conserve the nation's recreation resources.

Travel and food expenses are tax deductible. The co-sponsoring agency or group provides training, tools, and supervision. There is a non-refundable registration fee of $80 for American Hiking Society members and $100 for non-members.

Big City Mountaineers

Agency: Non Pro
Season: Summer
Contact: Marcus Moran
210 Beaver Brook Canyon Rd., Suite 200
Evergreen, CO 80439
E-mail: info@bigcitymountaineers.org
Web: www.bigcitymountaineers.org
Phone: (800) 644–2122

Description/Positions Available: Take an incredible eight-day trip with under-resourced urban teenagers into the mountains of Colorado, California, and Washington.

We are looking for adult leaders with backpacking experience and a desire to help urban teens. We also need local volunteers in Seattle, Denver, and San Francisco to work with BCM staff and coordinate trip logistics. This includes working with gear, purchasing and distributing food supplies, picking up volunteers from the airport, working with youth organizations to prepare their teens for our experiences, and helping with local media events.

National Park Service/Amtrak

Agency: National Park Service
Season: Summer
Contact: Please see individual listings for con-

tact information under the following states: Colorado, Illinois, Louisiana, Massachusetts, Missouri, Montana, New York, North Dakota, Oklahoma, and Texas.

Description/Positions Available: Trails & Rails is a partnership between the National Park Service and Amtrak to provide educational programs on passenger trains running through selected regions of the country. National Park Service sites that participate serve as host parks for each program and are responsible for the recruiting, training, and general administration of the local Trails & Rails program. These host sites can be found in various regions of the United States. National Park Service rangers and volunteers provide Amtrak passengers with information on significant natural and cultural sites, history, the environment, and the cultural diversity along each route. Programs are presented intermittently over the train's public address system and in other designated areas. Volunteers will "ride the rails" between local Amtrak stations and points along each route. Volunteers will be available to answer questions about the region, National Park Service sites along their Amtrak route, and the National Park Service. They will work with traveling displays and hand out literature. All volunteers selected for the Trails & Rails will be registered with the Volunteers in Parks (VIP) program. As a volunteer, you will not be paid by the federal government. However you will have the benefit of working with a national park, and there will be other rewards as well. You will meet people from all over the United States and abroad. You will have the opportunity to make the most of the talents that you have and will develop new skills and experiences that will enrich your life and assist you in present or future careers.

Volunteer Requirements: Trails & Rails volunteers must be flexible and adaptable to ever-changing situations and audiences. You should be comfortable speaking in public and working with different people. Volunteers are required to make at least three trips throughout the summer season. Most Trails & Rails programs involve a commitment of a full day in order to meet scheduling requirements. There are some programs across the country that may require two or three full days away from home, with overnight stays in hotels (the lodging costs are covered by the program). Volunteers must be at least eighteen years of age or, if not, work with a responsible adult. Volunteers should be in good health so that they can successfully carry out their volunteer duties and responsibilities. There are narrow stairs to climb on a moving train, and occasional heavy lifting is required. You will be reimbursed for necessary expenses associated with the program.

Trails & Rails volunteers are required to ride once a month between Williston, North Dakota, and Shelby, Montana. There are no housing, camping, or lodging facilities provided by the program. The only expenses covered are those associated with the actual program.

Passport in Time Clearinghouse

Agency: PIT
Season: Year-round
Contact: Jody Holmes
P.O. Box 31315
Tucson, AZ 85751-1315
E-mail: pit@sricrm.com
Web: www.passportintime.com/
Phone: (800) 281–9176

Description/Positions Available: This program, also known as "PIT," is a volunteer program inviting the public to share in the thrill of discovery through archaeological and historical research. Forest Service archaeologists and historians guide volunteers in activities ranging from archaeological excavations to historic building restoration. Projects vary in length from a weekend to a month. Many projects involve backcountry camping, for which volunteers must supply their own gear and food. Others offer meals for a small fee. Some provide hookups for RVs and trailers.

The *PIT Traveler*, a free newsletter announcing current projects, is published each year in March and September.

Student Conservation Association

Agency: SCA
Season: Year-round
Contact: Recruitment Office
P.O. Box 550
Charlestown, NH 03603
E-mail: internships@sca-inc.org
Web: www.sca-inc.org/vol/raca/raca.htm
Phone: (603) 543–1700

Description/Positions Available: Conservation interns are individuals eighteen years or older who volunteer their services through SCA for short- and long-term positions in exchange for training and experience. Conservation interns serve in twelve-week to twelve-month positions in federal, state, local, and private resource management sites all over the United States. If you want to make a difference while having an experience that may change your life, contact SCA.

Conservation interns assist with a full range of natural/cultural resource management- and conservation-related tasks in both field and office settings. They work in a variety of fields, including, Archaeology, Biological Sciences, Gis/Gps Computer Aided Drafting, Historical Studies, Environmental Education, Art and Graphic Design, Landscape Architecture, Recreation/ Wildlife/Resource Management, Forestry, and Ecological Restoration. The required qualifications vary according to the position.

Benefits: interns will receive a weekly living allowance, a travel grant, room and board, accident and/or medical coverage, supervision and training, as well as college credit. Participants may also be eligible to receive an AmeriCorps Education award from $1,180 for twelve-week positions to $4,725 for ten-month positions.

U.S. Army Corps of Engineers

Agency: United States Corps of Engineers
Season: Year-round
Contact: Volunteer Clearinghouse
P.O. Box 1070
Nashville, TN 37202
E-mail: Gayla.Mitchell@lrn02.usace.army.mil
Web: www.orn.usace.army.mil/volunteer
Phone: (800) 865–8337

Description/Positions Available: The U.S. Army Corps of Engineers is the steward of twelve million acres of land and water at 460 lakes and projects across the country. Volunteers play an important role in protecting natural resources and maintaining recreation facilities.

Volunteer opportunities include park and Campground Hosts, visitor center staff, and program conductors. We also need help cleaning shorelines, restoring fish and wildlife habitats, maintaining park trails and facilities, and more. A free campsite is often included.

Alaska

Alaska Public Lands Information Center, Fairbanks

Agency: National Park Service
Season: Year-round
Contact: Sabrina Dallegge
250 Cushman St., Suite 1-A
Fairbanks, AK 99701
E-mail: sabrina_dallegge@nps.gov
Web: aplic@nps.gov
Phone: (907) 456–0529

Description/Positions Available: The Alaska Public Lands Information Center in Fairbanks uses volunteers year-round in many exciting positions and projects. These include Visitor Use Assistant, working at the visitors desk meeting and greeting visitors, stocking merchandise in the Alaska

Natural History Association Gift Shop, assisting school children with Discovery Day projects and with special demonstration programs, operating audio and video equipment in the theater, and much more. Winter visitor hours begin on Labor Day, Tuesday through Saturday from 10:00 A.M. to 6:00 P.M. and changing to summer hours on Memorial Day Weekend, seven days a week from 9:00 A.M. to 6:00 P.M.

Current opportunities also include the following posts: Visitor Use Assistant, Audiovisual Technician, Special Projects Assistant, Administrative Clerk, Special Assistant to the Manager, and Interpretive Assistant.

Alaska State Parks

Agency: State parks
Season: Summer
Contact: Lynn Blessington, Volunteer Coordinator
550 W. 7th Ave, Suite 1380
Anchorage, AK 99501
E-mail: volunteer@dnr.state.ak.us
Web: www.alaskastateparks.org

Description/Positions Available: Alaska State Parks stretch from the rain forests and fjords of the southeast to the rolling hills and birch forests of the Interior—an area as vast and varied as the state itself. Volunteers can experience snow-capped mountains, untamed rivers, ice-blue glaciers, wilderness, and wildlife.

We need Ranger Assistants, Trail Crews, Natural History Interpreters, and Campground Hosts. Many positions provide rustic housing or camping, expense allowances, training, and uniforms. Minimum age is eighteen. You must be a U.S. citizen to apply. The application deadline is April 1, and a catalog with complete position descriptions is available on request or at our Web site.

Anchorage District Office, Bureau of Land Management

Agency: Bureau of Land Management
Season: Year-round

Contact: Volunteer Coordinator
6881 Abbott Loop Rd.
Anchorage, AK 99507
E-mail: nancy_stimson@blm.gov
Phone: (907) 267–1278

Description/Positions Available: Nestled in the heart of Anchorage lies the Bureau of Land Management's Campbell Tract. It is bordered on three sides by the Municipality of Anchorage's Far North Bicentennial Park and by modern neighborhoods to the west. Popular recreation trails are open for nonmotorized recreation: mountain biking, jogging, walking, cross-country skiing, skijoring, and dog mushing.

Volunteer opportunities include conducting visitor and resource surveys, monitoring wildlife, monitoring trail counters, picking up litter, and maintaining trail signs. Good public speaking skills will be helpful. You must live in the local area, as you will be compensated for mileage to and from work each day.

Bering Land Bridge National Preserve, Arctic West Parklands

Agency: National Park Service
Season: Summer
Contact: Volunteer Coordinator
P.O. Box 220
Nome, AK 99762
Phone: (907) 443–6101

Description/Positions Available: This preserve, a remnant of a land mass that connected Asia with North America and served as a migration route for people, animals, and plants, lies just below the Arctic Circle on the Seward Peninsula in northwest Alaska. Eskimos from neighboring villages pursue subsistence lifestyles and manage their reindeer herds in the preserve. The terrain includes tundra and many small lakes, streams and lagoons that support a variety of wildlife and plants. Most positions involve spending time in field camps and require good outdoor skills and the stamina to endure difficult conditions.

Resource Assistants are needed to assist preserve managers with subsistence management, resource management, interpretation, and general support. Some positions require the ability to live and work in field camps for varying lengths of time. Actual duties will depend on experience. Stipends and housing are available.

Bureau of Land Management, Glennallen Field Office

Agency: Bureau of Land Management
Season: Summer
Contact: Marcia Butorac, Outdoor Recreation Planner
P.O. Box 147
Glennallen, AK 99588
E-mail: Marcia_Butorac@ak.blm.gov
Web: www.glennallen.ak.blm.gov
Phone: (907) 822–3217

Description/Positions Available: Campground Hosts for four Bureau of Land Management Campgrounds are needed in the Copper River Valley and Denali Highway areas.

Chugach National Forest, Cordova District

Agency: U.S. Department of Agriculture Forest Service
Season: Summer
Contact: Dixon Sherman
P.O. Box 280
Cordova, AK 99574
E-mail: dsherman@fs.fed.us
Phone: (907) 424–7661

Description/Positions Available: Cordova is located on the eastern side of Prince William Sound, where there is no road access to the Alaskan interior. However, a jet air service flies daily, and marine ferry services operate four or five times a week. Population varies from 2,600 in winter to 5,000 in summer. The Copper River Delta, a major breeding/staging area for millions of waterfowl and shorebirds as well as moose, brown bears, and wolves, is located 6 miles east of Cordova.

Trail Crew volunteers are needed to construct and maintain the Cordova Ranger District trail system, including brushing, constructing water bars, and repairing bridges, puncheons, and signs. Other projects may also be involved. Free housing is provided, along with $23 per diem compensation. Transportation is provided from Seattle to Cordova as is return flight for sixty days' service or more. Forest Service Hosts are also needed from June to September for Child's Glacier Recreation Area. We provide free camping at a semi-remote site. Propane gas for the generator and water are provided, but there are no hookups or running water. Applicants must have their own RV or trailer. Round-trip ferry tickets from Valdez to Cordova are provided.

Chugach National Forest, Cordova District

Agency: U.S. Department of Agriculture Forest Service
Season: Memorial Day through Labor Day or a six-week commitment.
Contact: Chris Dunlap
P.O. Box 280
Cordova, AK 99574
E-mail: cdunlap@fs.fed.us
Phone: (907) 424–4733

Description/Positions Available: Childs Glacier Recreation Site is a very remote location 48 miles from Cordova on the Copper River. In this area the river is a quarter of a mile wide with the Childs Glacier on one side and the recreation site on the other. Cordova is located on the Gulf Coast of Alaska in the Eastern Prince William Sound.

We are offering opportunities for Volunteer Site Hosts. Applicants need their own RV to live in and a vehicle to drive during time off. The Forest Service will provide propane, gas for a generator, portable water, cleaning equipment and supplies, round-trip ferry tickets from Valdez to Cordova, gas mileage for 100 miles per week, communication radios, and a SAT phone. No running water, electricity, or telephone at this site. Support services are provided three to four times per week. Duties include being a resident care taker and protecting the recreation site, greeting visitors, providing information, cleaning a four-toilet outhouse, general maintenance of five picnic sites and five tent camping sites, and keeping records of number of vehicles and visitors. Childs Glacier receives approximately 7,000 visitors per summer. Hosts have two days off mid-week.

Gates of the Arctic National Park and Preserve

Agency: National Park Service
Season: Year-round
Contact: Roger Semler, Chief of Operations
P.O. Box 26030
Bettles, AK 99726
E-mail: GAAR_Visitor_Information@nps.gov
Web: www.nps.gov/gaar/
Phone: (907) 692–5494

Description/Positions Available: This park is located in Alaska's greater interior. There are four locations for job opportunities: Bettles Ranger Station and Visitor Center, Anaktuvuk Pass Ranger Station, Marion Creek–Coldfoot Visitor Center, and Fairbanks Headquarters. Prospective volunteers will find a variety of positions available. All positions are based on park-specific needs from season to season. These could include maintenance, interpretation, and/or backcountry patrols. Please visit the official National Park Service Web site www.nps.gov/volunteer to obtain an application.

Kenai Fjords National Park

Agency: National Park Service
Season: Summer
Contact: Doug Capra, VIP Coordinator
Seward, AK 99664
E-mail: Doug_Capra@nps.gov
Web: www.nps.gov/kefj/
Phone: (907) 224–3175

Description/Positions Available: One of the most accessible national parks in Alaska, Kenai Fjords National Park is located on Alaska's Kenai Peninsula, 130 road-miles southwest of Anchorage, accessible by bus, train, boat, and plane. The park encompasses approximately 669,000 acres, including rugged and glaciated mountains, 300 square miles of the Harding Icefield, glaciers, fjords, bays, and terrestrial and marine wildlife. Park headquarters and visitor center are located in Seward. Accessible by road, the Exit Glacier area is located approximately 12 miles from Seward where park visitors may walk a partly paved trail to the foot of the glacier. There is also a nature trail and overlook loop trail and the strenuous 3-mile Harding Icefield Trail that takes hikers through spruce and hemlock forests to heather-filled meadows, climbing well above treeline for a view of the icefield.

Opportunities are available between mid-June and September for trail reconstruction after snowmelt, routine maintenance, and Harding Icefield patrols. These positions will compensate the volunteer with $15 per diem. There is no housing available, but there are camping and RV areas along the Exit Glacier road within a short drive of the park.

Kodiak National Wildlife Refuge

Agency: U.S. Fish and Wildlife Service
Season: Year-round
Contact: Missy Epping
1390 Buskin River Rd.
Kodiak, AK 99615
E-mail: missy_epping@fws.gov
Web: www.r7.fws.gov/nwr/kodiak/kodnwr.html

Description/Positions Available: Kodiak Island lies in the Gulf of Alaska, south of Cook Inlet and Kenai Peninsula. The city of Kodiak is located near the northeastern tip of Kodiak Island, at the north end of Chiniak Bay. The Visitor Center is approximately 4.5 miles from the city of Kodiak. By air it is about one hour from Anchorage. By ferry from Homer it is a ten-hour journey. The average daily temperature is 54° in July and 30° in January. September, October, and May are the wettest months, averaging more than 6 inches of rain.

We are seeking two Visitor Center/ Environmental Educators. The volunteers for this position operate the Refuge Visitor Center and the Alaska Natural History Association outlet. Applicants must be able to welcome visitors, answer questions, and provide visitors with informative directions and literature concerning refuge lands, waters, and wildlife. They will also review and analyze the routine operation of the Visitor Center, assisting with special programs and events. Managing school visits and presenting interpretive talks will also be important parts of the volunteers' role.

Tongass National Forest, Admiralty National Monument

Agency: U.S. Department of Agriculture Forest Service
Season: Summer
Contact: John Neary
8461 Old Dairy Rd.
Juneau, AK 99801
E-mail: jneary@fs.fed.us
Web: www.fs.fed.us/r10/tongass/districts/ admiralty/frmain.htm
Phone: (907) 790–7481

Description/Positions Available: Known for its large concentration of bald eagles and brown bear populations, this monument is located on an island south of Juneau, accessible only by boat or floatplane. Most of the island is undeveloped and offers recreational opportunities such as hunting, fishing, boating, and bear-viewing. Elevations range from sea level to 3,500 feet, with temperatures ranging from the forties to the seventies in summer. Orientation will take place at the district office in Juneau, and volunteers will spend the rest of the field season on the island. Bunkhouse facilities are available in the Tlingit village of Angoon (population 750) or in Juneau (population 27,000).

A Wilderness Ranger is needed between April and early September. Familiarity with small boat operation and rifle handling is valuable, as are public contact skills. Work will include light trail maintenance and providing information to visitors. The volunteer will be in the field for ten days at a time. Benefits include food, a bunkhouse on days off, expenses, and round-trip travel upon completion of the field season. Apply by February 1.

Tongass National Forest, Petersburg District

Agency: U.S. Department of Agriculture Forest Service
Season: Summer
Contact: Volunteer Coordinator
P.O. Box 1328
Petersburg, AK 99833
Phone: (907) 772–3871

Description/Positions Available: Surrounded by the mountains and wildlife of Mitkof Island, Ohmer Creek Campground is a quiet site at the edge of an old-growth forest and a salt-water estuary, where streams abound seasonally with salmon, steelhead, and trout.

A Campground Host is needed between late May and August to perform light maintenance and cleaning as well as disseminate information to the public. Good people skills are essential. Applicants must have their own unit and personal transportation. There are no hookups available. A stipend may be provided.

Tongass National Forest, Sitka Ranger District

Agency: U.S. Department of Agriculture Forest Service
Season: Summer
Contact: Sandy Russell
201 Katlian, Suite 109
Sitka, AK 99835
E-mail: srussell03@fs.fed.us
Web: www.fs.fed.us/r10/tongass/
Phone: (907) 747–4216

Description/Positions Available: Location of these volunteer Campground Host positions is in beautiful and moody Southeastern Alaska at Sitka. Sitka is a remote town of about 9,000 people located on Baranof Island within the Alexander Archipelago off the British Columbia coast. Access to Sitka is by the Alaska Marine Highway out of Bellingham, Washington, or Prince Rupert, British Columbia, or by Alaska Airlines.

Opportunities are available for Volunteer Campground Hosts (two positions); retired couples preferred. Applicants must be available to be in Sitka May 1 through September 10. Duties include light maintenance; the daily opening and closing of the campground access gate; cleaning the campsites, fire rings, and restrooms; litter pick-up; splitting firewood rounds using a commercial log splitter; greeting and informing visitors and monitoring trail and campground use. You must be people oriented with good communication and language skills. Travel and living reimbursements are a possibility. You must provide your own self-contained living unit and be in good health. No pets please. Deadline for applying is March 15 or until positions are filled.

Arizona

Apache-Sitgreaves National Forest, Lakeside District

Agency: U.S. Department of Agriculture Forest Service
Season: Summer
Contact: Beth Puschel
RR 3, Box B-50
Lakeside, AZ 85929
E-mail: Bpuschel@fs.fed.us
Phone: (520) 368–5111

Description/Positions Available: This district stretches from the White Mountains to the edge of the Mogollon Rim country. Fish in one of the area's many lakes, hike in the canyon/Manzanita country, or cool off in high meadows surrounded by aspens. The area provides a seemingly remote experience, but it is close to the amenities of several White Mountain communities.

Campground Hosts are needed for small non-fee camp areas. This entails providing information to the public about area recreation opportunities and assisting with routine clean-up operations. Volunteers require a self-contained RV or trailer. No hookups are available. Reimbursement for propane is provided. Our season runs between Memorial Day and Labor Day. Apply by April 1. We are also looking for Trail Patrol and Maintenance volunteers at the White Mountain Trail System. The WMTS is a series of eleven connected loops totaling 180 miles that wind across the Lakeside District. Work includes visitor contact on heavily used trails and yearly maintenance, including clearing brush, cleaning water bars, and re-signing. Volunteers need a self-contained RV or trailer. No hookups are available. Reimbursement for propane is provided. A two- to three-month commitment is preferred. Here, the trail season runs between April and October. Applications are accepted throughout this season.

Buenos Aires National Wildlife Refuge

Agency: U.S. Fish and Wildlife Service
Season: Year-round
Contact: Bonnie Swarbrick
P.O. Box 109
Sasabe, AZ 85633
E-mail: bonnie_swarbrick@fws.gov
Web: www.fws.gov
Phone: (520) 823–4251, extension 116

Description/Positions Available: The Buenos Aires NWR is located 60 miles southwest of Tucson Arizona on the Mexican border. The Refuge is 117,000 acres comprised of semi-desert grassland, sky island, and desert riparian. The Refuge's management goals are to improve the condition of the native grassland, reestablish the endangered masked bobwhite quail, and provide a quality habitat for the hundreds of neo-tropical migratory birds that pass through each year, as well as the many mammal species that occur in this unique ecosystem.

Volunteer positions include work in the visitor center, public use work, light maintenance, equipment operation, and biology work. The Refuge provides housing, a stipend, and a vehicle (minimum of thirty-two hours per week with a three-month commitment).

Bureau of Land Management, Arizona State

Agency: Bureau of Land Management Office
Season: Year-round
Contact: Margaret Dwyer
222 N. Central Ave.
Phoenix, AZ 85004
E-mail: margedwyer@aol.com
Web: azwww.az.blm.gov/volunteer/volopps.html
Phone: (480) 515–1856

Description/Positions Available: There are limitless opportunities to make a difference on Arizona's public lands.

We are looking for Campground Hosts statewide, as well as various other opportunities. Each May we sponsor projects during Rivers Clean-up Day, and in June we provide support for statewide National Trails Day projects. Please visit our Web site, or give us a call for more information.

Bureau of Land Management, Kingman Field Office

Agency: Bureau of Land Management
Season: Year-round
Contact: Volunteer Coordinator
2475 Beverly Ave.
Kingman, AZ 86401

E-mail: kfoweb_az@blm.gov
Web: kingman.az.blm.gov/
Phone: (928) 692–4400

Description/Positions Available: The office is located in Northwestern Arizona and administers Burro Creek Campground in the Sonoran Desert and Wild Cow Springs Campground in the Hualapai Mountains (elevation 6,200 feet). Burro Creek features perennial pools surrounded by riparian vegetation and supports many types of outdoor recreation in a mild winter climate. Wild Cow Springs Campground, located in a mountain-top grove of ponderosa pine and oak trees, offers cooler mountain climates and a wide variety of recreation opportunities.

Campground Hosts are needed for Burro Creek Campground between October and April (water, sewer and P. V. electric provided); and at Wild Cow Springs Campground May through September, (water and P. V. electric provided). Duties include public contact, light maintenance, and ensuring fee compliance. A minimum two- to three-month commitment is required. Applicants must provide their own motor home or trailer. Benefits include waived camping fee and length-of-stay limit and training. Applications are accepted year-round.

Coronado National Forest, Sierra Vista Ranger District

Agency: U.S. Department of Agriculture Forest Service
Season: Summer
Contact: Mary Dalton
USDA/FS, Coronado NF, 5990 S. Hwy. 92
Hereford, AZ 85615
E-mail: mhdalton@fs.fed.us
Phone: (520) 378–0311

Description/Positions Available: Fire Lookouts are needed for the Red Mountain Lookout in the Patagonia mountains of southeastern Arizona. Volunteers staff the remote lookout station for five- to ten-day shifts, eight to eleven hours per shift. You will be trained to use "firefinder", topo maps and radio in order to report smoke and weather conditions to the Tucson dispatch for fire crew response. Applicants must have excellent eyesight, be in good physical shape, have a willingness to live in isolated conditions (couples welcome), and map/compass skills. Our lookout features a small two-story cabin surrounded by catwalk, elevation 6,700 feet, propane appliances, a pit toilet, no running water, two bunks. The view is spectacular; with lots of incredible hiking nearby during time off. An interest in weather and storm patterns in mountain topography is helpful.

We have one or two positions available for Lookout Trainees. These are available to single individuals or a couple. Volunteers must provide their own food and travel to and from Tucson, Arizona. On days off from the lookout shifts, the district can provide camping space near the town of Sierra Vista for an RV or tent, as well as a place to shower. Transportation to and from the lookout to Sierra Vista (70 miles) for days off is provided (the facility is located on extremely rough 4x4 trail). After one summer as a volunteer, you will be eligible for subsequent work as a paid lookout.

Glen Canyon National Recreation Area

Agency: National Park Service
Season: April–November
Contact: Rick Jones
P.O. Box 1507
Page, AZ 86040
Phone: (928) 608–6405

Description/Positions Available: The recreation area is located in Southern Utah and Northern Arizona alongside Lake Powell—the second-largest reservoir in the United States, with 196 miles of shoreline. Lake Powell is in the heart of the beautiful Colorado Plateau and red rock canyon country.

Volunteers are needed to work the Trash Tracker Program, a lakeshore cleanup effort run in cooperation with the park concessionaire, Aramark. Each week a new group of volunteers,

four people maximum, sets out on a houseboat to a remote location on the lake. The group works eight hours per day cleaning up the shoreline. The rest of the day may be used for swimming, hiking, fishing, photography, or any other recreational activities. Trips range from five to seven days in length, and volunteers are responsible for their own food.

Kaibab National Forest

Agency: U.S. Department of Agriculture Forest Service
Season: Year-round
Contact: John Smith
P.O. Box 324
Kanab, AZ 80041
Phone: (800) 972–8600

Description/Positions Available: Located in northwestern Arizona, this is a little heaven on earth. We need volunteers for trail maintenance and building in the Kanab Creek Wilderness.

Peaks and Mormon Lake Ranger Districts

Agency: U.S. Department of Agriculture Forest Service
Season: Summer
Contact: Nina Hubbard
5075 N. Hwy. 89
Flagstaff, AZ 86004
E-mail: nhubbard@fs.fed.us
Web: www.fs.fed.us/r3/coconino
Phone: (928) 527–8213

Description/Positions Available: Flagstaff is located in the scenic, volcanic highlands of Arizona. The city sits at the base (7,000 feet) of the beautiful San Francisco Peaks and the Kachina Peaks Wilderness Area. The Ranger Districts manage a variety of habitats including grasslands, scrub, lakes, forest and subalpine habitat. The elevation ranges from 6,000 feet along the Mogollon Rim to 12,643 feet on Humphreys Peak, the highest point in Arizona. The area is known for its mild summer weather, close proximity to five National Forest Wilderness Areas, four national parks/Monuments, and many local points of interest. Outdoor recreation is a local lifestyle and includes almost the entire spectrum of possibilities.

Volunteer opportunities are diverse. They include trail maintenance, trail construction, wilderness patrol (foot and horseback), front desk visitor information services, environmental education (primarily outdoors), grounds maintenance, facilities maintenance, sign/woodshop. Volunteer opportunities in areas other than those listed may be considered if there is a need (e.g. range tech, wildlife tech, etc.). Internships are possible, and proposals may be discussed with the District contact. Federal housing is not available with the exception of RV hookups for some positions (you supply your own RV).

Petrified Forest National Park

Agency: National Park Service
Season: One week in April
Contact: Karen Beppler-Dorn
P.O. Box 2217
Petrified Forest, AZ 86028
E-mail: karen_beppler@nps.gov
Web: www.nps.gov/pefo
Phone: (928) 524–6228

Description/Positions Available: Petrified Forest National Park is located in northeastern Arizona and features the world's largest and most colorful concentration of petrified wood. Included in the park's 93,533 acres are the multi-hued badlands of the Painted Desert.

The park is looking for five or six volunteers to work on two trail projects during April, 2002. The first project runs for three days and is intended to install new water bars. The second runs for two days in which volunteers will prepare an adjacent area to the park road for re-vegetation. The park provides free lodging consisting of dormitory-style three-bedroom houses with two baths and full-size kitchens.

Agency: National Park Service
Season: Summer
Contact: Karen Beppler-Dorn
P.O. Box 2217
Petrified Forest, AZ 86028
E-mail: karen_beppler@nps.gov
Web: www.nps.gov/pefo
Phone: (928) 524–6228

Description/Positions Available: Petrified Forest National Park is located in northeastern Arizona, approximately 70 miles west of Gallup, New Mexico, and 25 miles east of Holbrook, Arizona. Park Headquarters are located on Interstate 40 at exit 311. Climate conditions are generally hot, dry, and windy. The area is subject to sudden thunderstorm activity.

Two positions are available for Backcountry Resource Management Volunteers. The first is for late spring/early summer of 2002. The second is for late summer/early fall 2002. Shared housing is provided. A stipend of approximately $200 per week for ten weeks may be available. The volunteer will conduct backcountry resource management patrols. The purpose of these patrols will be to monitor natural and cultural resource conditions, report wildlife sightings, record and report resource impacts, and provide interpretive messages to backcountry visitors. Other duties may include backcountry trash collection, mapping using GPS/GIS equipment, and archeological site monitoring. The volunteer must be able to carry packs up to fifty lbs. in rough country. Overnight camping may be required, and desert survival skills are necessary. The ability to ride a horse is valuable but not required for the position.

Petrified Forest National Park

Agency: National Park Service
Season: Year-round
Contact: Janet Fernandez
P.O. Box 2217
Petrified Forest, AZ 86028

E-mail: janet_fernandez@nps.gov
Web: www.nps.gov/pefo
Phone: (928) 524–6228, extension 276 or 238

Description/Positions Available: Become a volunteer at Petrified Forest National Park, and use your skills to help preserve one of America's unique landscapes. Petrified Forest not only protects one of the world's largest concentrations of petrified wood but also reveals a picture of Triassic times, 225 million years ago, in the colorful layers of the Painted Desert. Our 93,533-acre park contains fossil evidence of ancient reptiles, amphibians and early dinosaurs alongside prehistoric cultures dating back over 10,000 years and historic structures/travelways. The high-plateau, short-grass prairie is home to a fascinating variety of animals, birds, and plants.

Volunteer opportunities are as diverse as the natural and cultural resources of the park. Volunteers are needed for every season. Housing is available but limited, especially in the summer. There are dormitory-style houses, an apartment, and some trailer spaces with hookups. A minimum workweek of thirty-two hours is required to be eligible for park housing.

Pipe Spring National Monument

Agency: National Park Service
Season: Year-round
Contact: Debra Judd
HC 65, Box 5
Fredonia, AZ 86022
E-mail: debra_judd@nps.gov
Web: www.nps.gov/pisp/
Phone: (928) 643–7105

Description/Positions Available: Pipe Spring is an intercultural site north of the Grand Canyon. The cold water springs were home to the Puebloan people, the Paiute Indians, and later Mormon settlers. The monument uses volunteers from fall through spring. If you enjoy history and a variety of duties, this may be the place for you. Limited housing may be available, as well as an off-park RV site. At 5,000 feet this is a high desert area

located between Grand Canyon, Zion, and Bryce Canyon. Primary duties are work at the visitor desk and interpretation.

Volunteers commonly work four days a week, eight hours a day. This is usually four hours at the visitor desk, two hours doing thirty-minute tours through the old stone fort, and thirty minutes cleaning and dusting the historic house interior. Weekends and holidays may be scheduled.

Saguaro National Park

Agency: National Park Service
Season: Year-round
Contact: Tom Danton
3693 S. Old Spanish Trail
Tucson, AZ 85730
E-mail: Tom_Danton@nps.gov
Web: www.nps.gov.sagu

Description/Positions Available: Saguaro National Park is adjacent to the city of Tucson Arizona, with a district of the park to the east and to the west of the city. There are no volunteer quarters or trailer pads in the park, but we are close to lots of Sonoran Desert wilderness with city conveniences.

Volunteers might help visitors to the visitor centers, conduct naturalist programs, participate in environmental education programs with children, perform clerical details, hike or ride the trails, assist with park maintenance, or help researchers conduct studies in the park. Jobs are tailored to current park needs and volunteers' interests and skills.

Tonto National Forest, Globe District

Agency: U.S. Department of Agriculture Forest Service
Contact: Quentin Johnson
Rte. 1, Box 33
Globe, AZ 85503
Phone: (520) 402–6200

Description/Positions Available: Mild temperatures make Oak Flat and Jones Water campgrounds popular sites year-round. Both camp-grounds are located at an elevation of 4,200 feet just outside Globe. Oak Flat Campground is nestled in live oak and shrub habitat along the intermittently flowing Queen Creek drainage. Cottonwood, sycamore and walnut trees shade the perennial creek, which runs through Jones Water Campground and provides unique wildlife-viewing opportunities.

Campground Hosts for Oak Flat and Jones Water campgrounds are needed year-round. You greet visitors and are responsible for campground maintenance but also are encouraged to develop and present interpretive programs and to initiate other service projects. RV space and propane are provided, but you must have your own RV. No water or power is available at the campground. Subsistence should not exceed $5.00 per diem, funding permitting. Volunteers are also needed May to September for the Pinal Mountain Recreation Area. Camping gear and equipment are provided. Finally, Trail Specialists are needed March to November to learn trail maintenance and construction skills while backpacking in remote settings.

Tonto National Forest, Pleasant Valley Ranger District

Agency: U.S. Department of Agriculture Forest Service
Season: Summer
Contact: Howard S. Okamoto
P.O. Box 450
Young, AZ 85554
E-mail: hokamoto@fs.fed.us
Web: www.fs.fed.us/r3/tonto/districts/pv/pv.htm

Description/Positions Available: The Airplane Flat Recreation Site has a 6,600-foot elevation, a mature stand of ponderosa pine and is situated near Canyon Creek. The Upper Canyon Creek Recreation Site shares all of these features, with the addition of a mix of both White and Douglas fir.

We are interested in recruiting Campground Host(s).

Tonto National Forest, Pleasant Valley Ranger District

Agency: U.S. Department of Agriculture Forest Service
Season: Year-round
Contact: Howard S. Okamoto
P.O. Box 450
Young, AZ 85554
E-mail: hokamoto@fs.fed.us
Web: www.fs.fed.us/r3/tonto/districts/pv/pv.htm

The Sierra Ancha Experimental Station is bisected by Parker Creek and is situated near the break between the desert and ponderosa pine transition zones. An abundance of vegetation (Arizona cypress, ponderosa pine, blackberry etc.) and geological formations can be experienced at the facility.

Tonto National Monument

Agency: National Park Service
Season: Year-round
Contact: Susan Hughes, Chief Ranger
HC 02, Box 4602
Roosevelt, AZ 85545
E-mail: susan_hughes@nps.gov
Phone: (520) 467–2241

Description/Positions Available: Located in the upper Sonoran Desert, 110 miles east of Phoenix near Roosevelt Lake, this monument preserves two major cliff dwellings and numerous other sites of the Salado Indians dated A.D. 1150–1450.

We are looking for an Information Desk Assistant to help at the visitor center and a Roving Interpreter to greet visitors and help with tours. There are also positions available for Administrative Assistants, who perform clerical work, and Maintenance Assistants, who help with painting, plumbing, janitorial work, carpentry, and/or trail work. Finally, we need a Photo File and Library Assistant to help organize photo/slide files, update library cards/procedures, and perform data entry. This requires an interest in archaeology (and people) and good physical conditioning. Temperatures over one-hundred degrees from

June through August are common. Benefits include housing (consists of one trailer and one or two pads for RV vehicles) and training.

Wupatki/Sunset Crater Volcano/Walnut Canyon National Monuments

Agency: National Park Service
Season: Year-round
Contact: Chris Cole
Rt. 3, Box 149
Flagstaff, AZ 86004
E-mail: chris_cole@nps.gov
Phone: (520) 526–0502

Description/Positions Available: Wupatki

National Monument, 40 miles north of Flagstaff, protects nearly 2,700 archaeological sites in a high-desert environment. Sunset Crater Volcano National Monument preserves the Sunset Crater Volcano and associated volcanic features in a ponderosa pine environment just 15 miles north of Flagstaff. Walnut Canyon National Monument, 7 miles east of Flagstaff, is home to numerous twelfth-century cliff dwellings. Volunteer duties include assisting in the operation of the Visitor Centers, conducting trail patrols, guided walks and talks, resource management projects, and performing maintenance, library, and museum work. Duties vary according to the skills and interests of the volunteers. Trailer hookups and shared housing are available. Applications are accepted, and positions are available year-round.

Arkansas

Buffalo National River

Agency: National Park Service
Season: Spring
Contact: D. Wilson
402 N. Walnut, Suite 136
Harrison, AR 72601
E-mail: BUFF_Information@nps.gov
Web: www.nps.gov/buff

Description/Positions Available: The site is a beautiful, unpolluted, and free-flowing river in the Arkansas Ozarks with opportunities for canoeing, hiking, fishing, and sightseeing. It is located in north-central Arkansas near Harrison.

Positions available involve Visitor Center desk assistance, work as Campground Hosts, and miscellaneous resource projects as they are identified.

Hot Springs National Park

Agency: National Park Service
Season: Year-round
Contact: Jeff Heitzman
P.O. Box 1860
Hot Springs, AR 71902

E-mail: jeff_heitzman@nps.gov
Web: www.nps.gov/hosp
Phone: (501) 624–3383, extension 640

Description/Positions Available: Rich in cultural and natural resources, this park was established in 1832 as the first federal reserve. Luxurious old bathhouses line historical Bathhouse Row and offer a glimpse of life in the early 1900s. The surrounding park and the Ouachita National Forest have hiking trails, campgrounds and lakes. Hot Springs, a city with a population of about 36,000, has all the amenities of a major city.

Visitor Center Aides are needed to assist with information desk operations, bookstore operations, and cultural resource management. Administrative Aides are required to assist with clerical duties, office-machine operation, and computer programming. Finally, we are looking for Campground Aides to perform minor maintenance and cleaning, assist with grounds and trail work, and provide information to campers. Some training and a campsite with full hookups are provided. Housing may be available.

Ouachita National Forest

Agency: U.S. Department of Agriculture Forest Service
Season: Summer
Contact: Don Koger
1603 Hwy. 71 North
Mena, AR 71953
E-mail: dkoger@fs.fed.us
Web: www.fs.fed.us/oonf

Description/Positions Available: The Visitor Information Station is located on the eastern end of the Talimena Scenic Drive (Highway 88), Mena, Arkansas. The Shady Lake Campground is located in the southern part of Polk County on FS Rd. 38, 3 miles off State Highway 246.

We require Hosts for both the Visitors Information Station and the Shady Lake Campground.

Ouachita National Forest

Agency: U.S. Department of Agriculture Forest Service
Season: Year-round
Contact: Sharon Hose
1603 Hwy. 71 North
Mena, AR 71953
E-mail: shose@fs.fed.us
Web: www.fs.fed.us/oonf

Description/Positions Available: Ouachita National Forest in the Mena and Oden Ranger Districts is located on the border of Polk and Montgomery Counties, southwest Arkansas.

Volunteers are needed to act as Hosts in the Recreation Area Campgrounds and Visitor Information Stations. We are also recruiting staff for the Rich Mountain Fire Tower, Trail Maintenance, and ATV Trails.

Pea Ridge National Military Park

Agency: National Park Service
Season: Year-round
Contact: Mary Davis
Box 700
Pea Ridge, AR 72751
E-mail: Mary_Cox_Davis@nps.gov
Web: www.nps.gov/peri/

Description/Positions Available: This battlefield commemorates the largest and most decisive Civil War battle west of the Mississippi River. Pea Ridge is considered to be one of the most pristine and best-preserved Civil War battlefields. The park's 4,300 acres of fields and forested areas contain abundant wildlife and are laced with hiking trails and historic traces.

We are looking for Interpretative Aides to act as guides at the historic Elkhorn Tavern. Volunteers will research, develop, and present interpretive talks to the visiting public. Visitor Use Assistants are also needed to staff the visitor center information desk. We use Guides to research, develop and lead nature walks. Volunteers must enjoy people and be able to communicate clearly with individuals and groups. The Elkhorn Tavern is open May through October. The visitor center opens year-round. Housing is not available, but a campground is located nearby. Applications are accepted anytime. A trailer pad and hookups are available.

California

Bureau of Land Management

Agency: Bureau of Land Management
Season: Year-round
Contact: Dallas Meeks
1661 S. 4th St.
El Centro, CA 92243
E-mail: dmeeks@ca.blm.gov
Web: www.blm.gov/nhp/index.htm

Description/Positions Available: The program is based in the California desert areas in Imperial County, and the southeast mountain areas of San Diego County.

We have opportunities in the fields of botany (plant monitoring), archeology (site monitoring), and recreational trail monitoring/inspection.

Bureau of Land Management, Barstow Field Office

Agency: Bureau of Land Management
Season: Year-round
Contact: Rose Foster
2601 Barstow Rd.
Barstow, CA 92311
E-mail: Rose_Foster@ca.blm.gov
Web: www.ca.blm.gov/barstow/volunteer.html
Phone: (760) 252–6011

Description/Positions Available: The Barstow Field Office covers the area between the northern boundary of Joshua Tree National Park and the southern boundary of Fort Irwin Military Reservation and stretches from the eastern boundaries of Death Valley National Park and of San Bernardino National Forest to the California/Nevada state line. Its total area is nearly three million acres.

We especially need trail maintenance and construction workers, Campground Hosts, maintenance assistants, and heavy equipment operators. More broadly, if you are interested in getting involved in another way, you name it, we need it.

Doublehead Ranger District

Agency: U.S. Department of Agriculture Forest Service
Season: Summer
Contact: Mike Kegg
P.O. Box 369
Tulelake, CA 96134
E-mail: mkegg@fs.fed.us
Phone: (530) 667–2246

Description/Positions Available: Medicine Lake recreation area is located in northeastern Siskiyou County. The elevation in this area is approximately 6,500 feet, and vegetation consists of lodgepole pine, red fir with an understory of snowbrush and manzanita. The area is well known for its geological features. The Recreation Area has four campgrounds with a total of seventy-four campsites.

Four volunteer Campground Hosts are needed to hand out brochures, give directions, perform light maintenance, clean restrooms, barbecue grills, and campfire rings, and be good hosts.

East Bay Municipal Utility District

Agency: State parks
Season: Year-round
Contact: Steve Diers
Ebmud-M/S Mok—Pardee Center
Valley Springs, CA 95252
E-mail: sdiers@ebmud.com
Web: www.r5.fs.fed.us/stanislaus/calaveras/mcct

Sierra Foothills—Amador and Calaveras Counties—Pardee and Camanche Reservoir watersheds. Building a local segment of the Mokelumne Coast to Crest Trail (MCCT). The MCCT will eventually link the Pacific Crest Trail (Sierras) with the San Francisco Bay Area. EBMUD is a participant in this valuable effort.

Trail construction volunteers needed. Projects,

accomplished in four- to six-hour (Saturday) work-days scheduled for up to twice each month, corresponding with seasons and special events. Projects may include trail construction, erosion control, native plant restoration, habitat enhancement, and other land stewardship work. Annual activities are planned for education and volunteer appreciation. This is an enjoyable and satisfying activity for volunteers of all ages. Persons under eighteen years of age must have written permission from parent/guardian and those under sixteen must be accompanied by an adult. Projects are one-day activities only and therefore no housing, meals, or financial compensation are provided.

Eugene O'Neill National Historic Site

Agency: National Park Service
Season: Year-round
Contact: Volunteer Coordinator
P.O. Box 280
Danville, CA 94526
E-mail: EUON_Interpretation@nps.gov
Web: www.nps.gov/euon
Phone: (925) 838–0249

Description/Positions Available: Tao House is located on the outskirts of Danville in the San Ramon Valley, 30 miles east of San Francisco. The site is in the foothills of Las Trampas East Bay Regional Park, and across the valley from Mount Diablo State Park. Open grasslands and oak trees dot the surrounding landscape.

Eugene O'Neill, the only Nobel Prize–winning playwright from the United States and the architect of modern American theater, lived at Tao House in the hills above Danville from 1937 to 1944. It was at this site that he wrote his final and most successful plays, including *The Iceman Cometh, Long Days Journey Into Night,* and *A Moon For the Misbegotten.* Since 1980, the National Park Service has been restoring Tao House, its courtyard, and orchards, and telling the story of O'Neill, his work, and his influence on American theater.

The house and park need a Cultural Landscape Gardener. Your role will be to assist in restoring and preserving the historical gardens and landscape of Eugene O'Neill's Tao House property (Taoist courtyard and/or nut orchards). Useful skills for this position include an interest in gardening and being outdoors, the ability to work under minimal supervision, and a willingness to develop skills in preserving historic and cultural landscapes. Benefits include free admission to onsite productions, and volunteer field trips and ongoing training are provided. There is no housing available. Personal transportation is required (car, bike, walk).

Golden Gate National Recreation Area

Agency: National Park Service
Season: Year-round
Contact: Volunteer Coordinator
Fort Mason, Bldg. 201
San Francisco, CA 94123
E-mail: goga_volunteers@hotmail.com
Web: www.nps.gov/goga/vip/
Phone: (415) 561–4755

Description/Positions Available: Be a Park Hero! You can learn new skills, teach others, and stay active and involved. Volunteers at Golden Gate National Recreation Area help present the diverse resources of one of America's most popular national parks to today's visitors and help preserve these precious resources for future generations. Volunteer opportunities at Golden Gate National Recreation Area are as diverse as the natural and cultural resources of the park. History buffs, amateur naturalists, artists, students, gardeners and many more people have found a place to share their skills at Golden Gate. Each volunteer's contribution makes a big difference!

Volunteers at Golden Gate play a vital role in almost all aspects of park operations: collecting data on birds of prey at the premier hawk watching site on the west coast; designing and conducting information programs for the general public and school children; removing nonnative plants, growing native plants, and working in one of the park's nurseries; restoring historic structures such as a World War II barracks or a mess hall; working with park scientists to protect endangered species like the mission blue butterfly and peregrine falcon. Due to the number of volunteer and internship opportunities available, those who are interested are asked to visit our Volunteers in Parks Web site for a current listing and online application form.

Humboldt-Toiyabe National Forest

Agency: U.S. Department of Agriculture Forest Service
Season: Summer
Contact: Margaret Wood
HCA 1, Box 1000
Bridgeport, CA 93517
E-mail: mwood@fs.fed.us
Web: www.fs.fed.us/htnf/
Phone: (760) 932–7070

Description/Positions Available: Bridgeport Ranger District, Hoover, Carson Iceberg and Mokelumne Wildernesses.

We need two volunteers to complete wilderness recreation use monitoring. Volunteers will be working in the wilderness for five days, backpacking and camping, and collecting recreation use information and campsite inventories.

Indian Grinding Rock State Historic Park

Agency: State parks
Contact: Park Ranger
14881 Pine Grove-Volcano Rd.
Pine Grove, CA 95665
Web: www.parks.ca.gov/
Phone: (209) 296–7488

Description/Positions Available: This park derives its name from the grinding rock, the largest bedrock mortar in North America with associated petroglyphs. Located in the foothills

of the Sierra Nevada in the heart of the Mother-Lode gold historic area, this park supports mixed pine forest and open meadows. It is the setting for a reconstructed Indian village and includes the largest ceremonial "round house" in California. Other features of this park include trails, picnic sites, a campground and a regional Indian Museum.

A Campground Host is needed to operate the twenty-three-unit campground. A campsite with water, sewer and electrical hookups is provided in exchange for approximately twenty hours of work per week.

Inyo National Forest

Agency: U.S. Department of Agriculture Forest Service
Season: Summer
Contact: Susan Kranz or Pennie Custer
P.O. Box 148
Mammoth Lakes, CA 93546
E-mail: skranz@fs.fed.us
Web: www.r5.fs.fed.us/inyo
Phone: (760) 924–5515

Description/Positions Available: Mammoth Lakes, California, is located in the eastern Sierra adjacent to the Ansel Adams and John Muir Wilderness Areas.

Volunteers are needed for winter and summer in the Ranger Station and Visitor Center. The work is primarily staffing the information desk, ringing up bookstore sales, reporting on trail and road conditions, and a limited involvement in interpretive programs outside. Volunteer work is needed on weekends and holidays. There are also opportunities for volunteering with the interpretive ski program in the winter and assisting at the Visitor Center dispensing information.

Lake Tahoe Basin, Management Unit

Agency: U.S. Department of Agriculture Forest Service

Season: Year-round
Contact: Michael St Michel
870 Emerald Bay Rd., Suite 1
South Lake Tahoe, CA 96150
E-mail: Mstmichel@fs.fed.us
Phone: (530) 573–2611

Description/Positions Available: Interpretive Naturalists Volunteers are needed for the Tallac Historic Site and Lake Tahoe Visitor Center. Benefits include training and barracks housing; some positions also offer a stipend. Apply by April 1 for summer (June to September) positions. Two winter positions are also available between January and March for Interpretive Naturalists to assist with "Winter Trek," a winter environmental-education program. Training, uniform, and free government housing on the shores of Lake Tahoe are all provided. Up to $20 per diem subsistence is available. Apply by November 15. Finally, two Environmental Education Assistants are needed between September and mid-November to work with the Kokanee salmon environmental-education program. Apply by July 15.

Lassen Volcanic National Park

Agency: National Park Service
Season: Winter
Contact: Nancy Bailey
P.O. Box 100
Mineral, CA 96063
E-mail: nancy_bailey@nps.gov
Web: www.nps.gov/lavo/
Phone: (530) 595–4444, extension 5133

Description/Positions Available: This 106,000-acre national park located in northern California features bubbling mudpots, steaming fumaroles and boiling springs. The area is also rich in cultural and natural history.

We are in need of Interpretation and Cultural Resources Volunteers for visitor contact stations. You will be expected to sell publications, provide information, answer telephones, and possibly,

assist with snowshoe walks. We also need staff to assist with the library, museum, and photographic collections.

Lassen Volcanic National Park

Agency: National Park Service
Season: Summer
Contact: Nancy Bailey
P.O. Box 100
Mineral, CA 96063
E-mail: nancy_bailey@nps.gov
Web: www.nps.gov/lavo/
Phone: (530) 595–4444, extension 5133

Description/Positions Available: This 106,000-acre national park located in Northern California features bubbling mudpots, steaming fumaroles and boiling springs. The area is also rich in cultural and natural history.

Campground Hosts are required to greet campers, provide information, and check compliance. We also need Maintenance Volunteers for litter removal, historic building restoration, revegetation of disturbed areas, special construction projects, sign inventory, and trail maintenance. Interpretation and Cultural Resources Volunteers will be given the task of manning visitor contact stations, selling publications, providing information and answering telephones. Your role may possibly involve visitor activities. You will also assist with library, museum, and photograph collections. Natural Resources Management Volunteers may be involved in research and monitoring projects, including songbird, carnivore, small mammal, and amphibian baseline inventories.

Lava Beds National Monument

Agency: National Park Service
Season: Summer
Contact: Deborah Savage
Box 867
Tulelake, CA 96134
E-mail: Deborah_savage@nps.gov

Web: www.nps.gov/labe
Phone: (530) 667–2282

Description/Positions Available: Located in northeast California, Siskiyou county, near the Oregon border. The nearest large town is Klamath Falls, Oregon, 50 miles to the north.

Volunteers are needed to serve as Campground Hosts from Memorial Day to Labor Day. Volunteers must provide their own RV.

Los Padres National Forest, Forest Supervisors Office

Agency: U.S. Department of Agriculture Forest Service
Contact: Jeff Saley
6755 Hollister Ave., Suite 150
Goleta, CA 93117
E-mail: jsaley@fs.fed.us
Web: www.fs.fed.us/recreation/forest_descr/ca_r5_lospadres.html

Description/Positions Available: Volunteers are needed for each of the following: Staff Support Team; Outdoor Santa Barbara Visitor Center Representatives; Forest Visitor Information Assistant, and Fire Management Interns.

Los Padres National Forest, Monterey Ranger District

Agency: U.S. Department of Agriculture Forest Service
Contact: William Metz
406 S. Mildred
King City , CA 93930
E-mail: wmetz@fs.fed.us
Web: www.fs.fed.us/recreation/forest_descr/ca_r5_lospadres.html

Description/Positions Available: We need volunteers for Trail Maintenance and Watering Device Installation. No special skills are required for these jobs, and training is provided.

Los Padres National Forest, Mount Pinos Ranger District

Agency: U.S. Department of Agriculture Forest Service
Contact: John Kelly
34580 Lockwood Valley Rd.
Frazier Park, CA 93225
E-mail: jhkelly@fs.fed.us
Web: www.fs.fed.us/recreation/forest_descr/ca_r5_lospadres.html

Description/Positions Available: Volunteers are needed for each of the following: breeding bird surveys; trail maintenance; campground maintenance; wilderness patrol; spotted owl and goshawk surveys; range fence construction; sensitive plant surveys; tree seedling planting; silvicultural data collection; mistletoe pruning.

Los Padres National Forest, Santa Barbara Ranger District

Agency: U.S. Department of Agriculture Forest Service
Contact: Kerry Kellogg
3505 Paradise Rd.
Santa Barbara, CA 93105
E-mail: kkellogg@fs.fed.us
Web: www.fs.fed.us/recreation/forest_descr/ca_r5_lospadres.html
Phone: (805) 967–3481, extension 231

Description/Positions Available: Volunteer Wilderness Rangers and trail maintenance workers are always needed.

Midpeninsula Regional Open Space District

Agency: NON PRO
Season: Year-round
Contact: Paul Mckowan, Volunteer Coordinator
330 Distel Circle
Los Altos, CA 94022
E-mail: volunteer@openspace.org
Web: www.openspace.org

Description/Positions Available: The Mid-peninsula Regional Open Space District (MROSD) is an independent special district created in 1972 by the voters of northwestern Santa Clara County. It was joined in 1976 by southern San Mateo County, and later in 1992 the District annexed a portion of Santa Cruz County. MROSD has preserved more than 45,000 acres of public land and manages twenty-four open space preserves within its boundaries from San Carlos to Los Gatos. The District's mission is to acquire and preserve a regional greenbelt of open space land in perpetuity; protect and restore the natural environment; and provide opportunities for ecologically sensitive public enjoyment and education.

The goal of the volunteer program is to encourage active public participation in the maintenance, restoration, and protection of the District's natural resources, and provide cultural, historical, and environmental education opportunities to the public.

Modoc National Forest, Doublehead District

Agency: U.S. Department of Agriculture Forest Service
Season: Summer-Fall
Contact: Mike Kegg
P.O. Box 369
Tulelake, CA 96134
E-mail: mkegg@fs.fed.us
Phone: (530) 667–2246

Description/Positions Available: Medicine Lake is located in the northeastern portion of California with elevations around 6,700 feet. The accessible campgrounds are fairly remote, as the surrounding towns are 40 to 50 miles away.

Campground Hosts and Maintenance Workers needed for four developed campgrounds. The Forest Service will furnish a trailer pad and propane. Season begins approximately mid-May and ends mid-October. Daytime temperatures in the eighties; evenings are cool.

Needles Field Office

Agency: Bureau of Land Management
Season: Winter
Contact: Elaine Downing
101 W. Spikes Rd.
Needles, CA 92363
E-mail: elaine_downing@ca.blm.gov
Web: www.ca.blm.gov/needles
Phone: (760) 326–7003

Description/Positions Available: You will operate within the Needles Field Office jurisdiction, located at the eastern end of San Bernardino County—an area containing eighteen wilderness areas.

We are looking for Wilderness Volunteers to help monitor all wilderness areas. The job consists mostly of driving the boundaries, annotating any human activities that are noticed, and replacing carsonite signs. Some hiking is also required. Volunteers need to be able to carry a small daypack of fifteen to twenty lbs. and provide good hiking boots.

Needles Field Office

Agency: Bureau of Land Management
Season: Winter
Contact: Elaine Downing
101 W. Spikes Rd.
Needles, CA 92363
E-mail: elaine_downing@ca.blm.gov
Web: www.ca.blm.gov/needles
Phone: (760) 326–7003

Description/Positions Available: You will be operating within the Needles Field Office jurisdiction—on the eastern end of San Bernardino County at various isolated springs. Hiking is required. You must be able to carry at least thirty lbs. and be willing to camp at spike camps and at work sites. Bring your own camping gear, including good hiking boots. We recommend a minimum four-inch high-top boot. Other tools will be provided. Some reimbursement is available for meals.

The positions with the most demand are in the

areas of general labor, camp help, and assisting the staff in Tamarisk Removal projects. These opportunities are available between February and March 2002.

Pacific Crest Trail Association

Agency: NON PRO
Season: Summer–Fall
Contact: Volunteer Coordinator
5325 Elkhorn Blvd., MS #256
Sacramento, CA 95842–2526
E-mail: into@pcta.org
Web: www.pcta.org
Phone: (916) 349–2109

Description/Positions Available: The Pacific Crest Trail Association (PCTA) has many exciting opportunities for volunteers to get involved in the maintenance and reconstruction of the nation's premier long-distance hiking and equestrian path, the 2,650-mile-long Pacific Crest National Scenic Trail (PCT). Projects are located in some of the most scenic national forests, national parks, state parks, state forests and Bureau of Land Management Resource Areas in California, Oregon, and Washington.

The PCTA works in cooperation with the U.S. Forest Service, National Park Service, Bureau of Land Management, California State Parks, other agencies, many trail and conservation groups, and private landowners to promote, protect, and help maintain the PCT. Opportunities include: Adopt-A-Trail Program, Weekend Projects (one to four days), and Service Trips (five to ten days). While most efforts occur during the summer and fall months, some projects in southern California extend into the winter and spring. More information on PCTA's volunteer opportunities can be obtained by contacting the PCTA. Projects are also listed, as they are approved, on the PCTA Web site.

Point Reyes National Seashore

Agency: National Park Service
Season: Year-round

Contact: Tom Echols
Point Reyes National Seashore
Point Reyes Station, CA 94956
E-mail: tom_echols@nps.gov
Web: www.nps.gov/pore/involved/involved.htm
Phone: (415) 464–5195

Description/Positions Available: The Point Reyes National Seashore Volunteers in Parks are enthusiastic people who protect native ecosystems and improve recreational and interpretive opportunities by removing invasive nonnative plants, repairing streams, monitoring wildlife, repairing trails, and performing outreach to the public. Volunteers work in various settings throughout the park. Be sure to visit our Web site for detailed information!

Our main areas of recruitment include the following posts: rail repair and maintenance, adopt-a-trail, habitat restoration, harbor seal monitor, elephant seal docent, salmon monitoring and creek restoration, Native American village assistant, visitor center docent, rare plant monitoring, Morgan Horse Ranch assistant, tule elk docent, administrative assistant, snowy plover docent.

Redwood National and State Parks

Agency: National Park Service
Season: Year-round
Contact: Cathy Morris
1111 Second St.
Crescent City, CA 95531
E-mail: cathy_morris@nps.gov
Web: www.nps.gov/redw/index.htm
Phone: (707) 464–6101

Description/Positions Available: Work within the parks around the world's tallest living organisms and along the Pacific Coast. Weather will range from cool and rainy to sunny.

Trail crews work year-round in the parks. Due to the threatened and endangered species within the park, a measurable amount of work needs to be done by non-powered tools.

Santa Monica Mountains National Recreation Area

Agency: National Park Service
Season: Year-round
Contact: Mike Malone
401 W. Hillcrest Dr.
Thousand Oaks, CA 91360
E-mail: Mike_Malone@nps.gov
Web: www.nps.gov/samo

Description/Positions Available: There are positions available in the following areas: trail maintenance, removal of invasive plants, and maintenance of revegetated sites.

Sonoma Coast State Beach, Salt Point State Park, Armstrong Redwoods State Reserve

Agency: State parks
Season: Year-round
Contact: Elizabeth Haskell, Program Coordinator
Stewards Of Slavianka, P.O. Box 221
Duncans Mills, CA 95430
E-mail: sos@mcn.org
Web: www.stewardsofslavianka.org
Phone: (707) 869–9177

Description/Positions Available: Sonoma Coast State Beach features 19 miles of coastline on Highway 1 north of Bodega Bay. Salt Point State Park, located on Highway 1, 19 miles north of Jenner, features coastline and forest. Armstrong Redwoods State Reserve, located in Guerneville, California, is an old growth Redwood park.

Whale Watchers are needed on weekends between December and May at Bodega Head to educate the public about gray whale migration. Seal Watchers are also needed, especially March through September, at Goat Rock State Beach to educate the public about California harbor seals. Hosts are needed for the Jenner and Armstrong

Visitor Centers to provide information to the public about the natural and cultural history of the area. We are also recruiting Sonoma Coast tour guides for Tide Pool and Watershed Education programs. Finally, trail and firewood crews are needed at Salt Point State Park and Redwoods State Reserve. Junior Ranger Program leaders are also needed.

Stone Lakes National Wildlife Refuge

Agency: U.S. Fish and Wildlife Service
Season: Year-round
Contact: Amy Hopperstad
1624 Hood-Franklin Rd.
Elk Grove, CA 95758
E-mail: amy_hopperstad@fws.gov
Phone: (916) 775–4416

Description/Positions Available: Stone Lakes National Wildlife Refuge is located south of Sacramento, outside the city of Elk Grove. This urban refuge provides important riparian, wetland, and grassland habitat for many local resident species, as well as migrant birds along the Pacific Flyway. Public access is limited and the refuge staff is small, so the refuge depends on dedicated volunteers to help with environmental education, bird banding, habitat restoration, and special events.

Volunteer opportunities for leading school and public group tours, habitat restoration, bird banding, office work, maintenance, special events, and additional special projects. Volunteers are required to go through one of the two annual volunteer training sessions in spring or fall.

Trinity Alps Wilderness Area

Agency: U.S. Department of Agriculture Forest Service
Season: Summer
Contact: Jim Holmes
P.O. Box 1190
Weaverville, CA 96093

E-mail: MountainJoe@TDS.net
Web: www.r5.fs.fed.us/shastatrinity/
Phone: (530) 286–2860

Description/Positions Available: Located in northern California between Redding (in the Central Valley) and Eureka (on the coast), the Trinity Alps Wilderness is the second largest wilderness in the state. It contains 512,000 acres with 700 miles of trails—and offers unlimited backcountry opportunities. Its virgin forests are covered with Douglas fir, incense cedar, white fir, sugar pine, ponderosa pine, madrone, oak, big tooth maple, aspen, and alder—and those are just the dominant species. Heavily glaciated in the last ice age, the Alps have been left with more than seventy spectacular Alpine Lakes. The high mountain meadows offer incomparable flower shows starting in May at the lower elevations and lasting into October at higher elevations. The Wilderness is a six-hour drive to the nearest large metropolitan area (San Francisco). Consequently, most hikers are overnight users, and usage is relatively low by California standards.

Wilderness Patrol Persons are needed from May through September. This is a volunteer position that compensates the volunteer with $22 per diem. A typical Wilderness Patrol tour runs from Wednesday to Wednesday (eight-day tours) followed by six days off. Volunteers spend their eight-day tours backpacking on assigned routes making visitor contacts and maintaining backcountry campsites. All Patrolmen are delivered to the trailhead with Forest Service radios in Forest Service vehicles (sparing your rig Trailhead dirt roads!). All state-of-the-art backpacking gear and stove fuel are supplied by the Forest Service. Additionally, accommodations for the season are provided for free in the barracks at the Weaverville Ranger District in historic Weaverville. Weaverville is the county seat of Trinity County and was the inspiration for "Shangri-La" in the movie *Lost Horizons*. It is a charming mountain town of 3,600 permanent residents. This volunteer position is a real "sleeper". If you can afford to get along on the per diem for the season, this is an unparalleled opportunity. Contact Jim Holmes at the Weaverville Ranger District (530–623–1766) or at home (530–286–2860).

Whiskeytown National Recreation Area

Agency: National Park Service
Season: Year-round
Contact: Phyllis Swanson
P.O. Box 188
Whiskeytown, CA 96095
E-mail: phyllis_swanson@nps.gov
Web: www.nps.gov/whis

Description/Positions Available: Located on California Highway 299 off I–5 near Redding, California, Whiskeytown National Recreation Area—with its mountainous backcountry and man-made large reservoir—offers many summer activities such as hiking and boating as well as the historical remains of buildings erected during the California Gold Rush of 1849. Whiskeytown Lake, with 36 miles of shoreline and covering 3,200 acres, is excellent for most water-related activities, including swimming, scuba diving, water skiing, boating, and fishing.

Visitor Center volunteers assist in staffing the Visitor Center by providing information, answering questions about the area, providing directions, and selling park entrance fee passes. Training provided. Campground Hosts are stationed at Brandy Creek RV Campground. They assist staff by maintaining the RV campground and Brandy Creek picnic area and beach facilities, assist visitors to the RV campground, picnic area and beaches by answering questions about fees and opportunities in the area. Other volunteer opportunities involve tree planting, watershed restoration, exotic plant removal, surveys, and ground maintenance. Please call for an application or to get more information.

Colorado

Barr Lake State Park

Agency: State parks
Season: Year-round
Contact: Mary Barnell
13401 Picadilly Rd.
Brighton, CO 80601
Phone: (303) 659–6005

Description/Positions Available: A premier bird-watching area, home to more than 330 species of birds, Barr Lake is a reservoir on the high plains. We offer activities including wildlife-viewing, limited boating, fishing, hiking, and picnicking.

A Volunteer Naturalist is needed to assist with guided nature walks for school groups, organizations, and the general public and to serve as an Information Specialist on weekends. Other duties involve assisting with programs for senior citizens and physically handicapped people. Benefits include extensive training in natural history and interpretive techniques. Year-round position. Hours vary. After forty-eight hours of volunteer service, volunteers receive a free state parks pass. Training is provided. Many other opportunities exist, including gardening, animal care, and newsletter production.

Bureau of Land Management, Glenwood Springs Field Office

Agency: Bureau of Land Management
Season: Summer
Contact: Dorothy Morgan
P.O. Box 1009
Glenwood Springs, CO 81602
E-mail: Dorothy_Morgan@co.blm.gov
Web: www.co.blm.gov/gsra/gshome.htm

Description/Positions Available: Western Slope of Colorado, along I-70 between Vail and Rifle. The area covers diverse terrain such as open sage fields, Pinyon-Juniper woodland, and lush forests. Recreational opportunities include rafting on the Colorado, Eagle and Roaring Fork Rivers, camping, hiking, and mountain biking.

Campground Host, Tamarisk removal (groups only), Trash Clean-up (groups only).

Colorado Mountain Club

Agency: NON PRO
Season: Year-round
Contact: Sarah
710 10th St. #200
Golden, CO 80401
E-mail: peters@cmc.org
Web: www.cmc.org/cmc
Phone: (800) 633–4417, extension 112

Description/Positions Available: Your headquarters is Golden, Colorado, but the location of sites for trail work may vary.

We are looking for year-round Conservation Interns and Seasonal Trail Crew volunteers.

Florissant Fossil Beds National Monument

Agency: National Park Service
Season: Summer
Contact: Volunteer Coordinator
P.O. Box 185
Florissant, CO 80816
E-mail: FLFO_Information@nps.gov
Web: www.nps.gov/flfo
Phone: (719) 748–3253

Description/Positions Available: We offer Summer Internships in Interpretation, Paleontology and Resource Management.

Interpretive Interns provide information to the public about the fossil resources and the natural and cultural history of the area. Following a training period, they plan, prepare, and present programs to groups of all ages; conduct guided hikes; contact visitors on the trails; give historic homestead tours; staff the visitor center; and sell publications. Other duties will be assigned according to the interns' interests and may include: natural resource management, fossil excavation, developing interpretive media, and wildland fire fighting. Interns will gain insight into park operations, including administration, maintenance, and protection. Interpretive interns are supervised by the Interpretive Ranger. Interpretive Intern applicants will be evaluated in the following areas: ability or interest in developing communication and public speaking skills; ability to work with a variety of people of all ages; ability to work independently and as part of a team; and interest and ability to work outdoors. There are no specific educational requirements, but basic knowledge of natural sciences or geology is desirable.

Paleontology interns will work on projects relating to the geological and paleontological resources of the park. Typical roles including fossil collection and curation; technical assistance with excavating, inventorying and monitoring of sites; database development; and self-directed research. The specific scope of duties will be determined by the needs of the park and the interns' area of interest. Self-initiated research projects require a research proposal outlining the project and specific fieldwork to be conducted. Paleontology interns are supervised by the parks' Paleontologist. Paleontology intern applicants must have completed basic undergraduate course work for a degree in geology or biology. Preference will be given to students starting graduate or undergraduate thesis/dissertation projects. Professional applicants already holding degrees will also be considered.

Resource Management interns will work on projects relating to the biological and physical resources of the park. Roles include weed management, water quality monitoring, fire management, vegetation and wildlife monitoring, and restoration and revegetation activities. Interns will gain insight into all areas of park operations and management, including administration, mainte-

nance, and protection. Resource Management interns are supervised by the Chief Ranger. Resource Management interns must have completed basic undergraduate coursework for a degree in biology and have the interest and ability to work outdoors.

All interns must be available for the weeklong training period starting May 28. Paleontology and Resource Management interns may begin their term prior to this date. Starting or ending dates may be negotiated. Other volunteer positions may be arranged at other times of the year. Reimbursement of expenses and housing are usually available for summer internships only. To apply for Interpretive and Resource Management Internships, mail a resume with the phone numbers of at least two references, a copy of academic transcripts, and a cover letter that states why you are interested in the position. Applications for the Paleontology Internship should include a resume, a copy of academic transcripts, two professional letters of reference, and a cover letter outlining the applicant's specific interests. A research proposal is required for those interested in self-initiated research projects. The deadline for summer 2002 applications is March 16, 2002. Selections are made in April, after telephone interviews and reference checks. If you wish to be considered for more than one of the internships, please send separate applications.

Grand Mesa, Uncompahgre, and Gunnison National Forests, Gunnison Ranger District

Agency: U.S. Department of Agriculture Forest Service
Season: Summer
Contact: Michael Jackson
216 N. Colorado
Gunnison, CO 81230
E-mail: mdjackson@fs.fed.us
Phone: (970) 642–4401

Description/Positions Available: Volunteers are needed for a variety of wildlife survey work in late spring and summer in the southern Colorado Rockies near the Continental Divide. One to four positions will be offered and candidates with knowledge of wildlife and bird species will be given priority.

Great Sand Dunes National Monument

Agency: National Park Service
Season: Year-round
Contact: Libbie Landreth
11999 Hwy. 150
Mosca, CO 81146
E-mail: libbie_landreth@nps.gov
Web: www.nps.gov/grsa/

Description/Positions Available: Rising to heights of 750 feet, the Great Sand Dunes are the tallest dunes in North America. The dunes are nestled between two mountain ranges of the Rocky Mountains, the Sangre de Cristos and the San Juans.

Volunteers are needed for visitor center operations and information services, interpretation, trail maintenance, museum (curatorial experience preferred). We also need Librarians and Campground Hosts. Benefits include training, supervision, uniform, and housing (in most instances). College credit can be arranged.

Gunnison Ranger District

Agency: U. S. Department of Agriculture Forest Service
Season: Summer
Contact: Gay Austin
216 N. Colorado
Gunnison, CO 81230
E-mail: gaustin@fs.fed.us
Phone: (970) 642–4406

Description/Positions Available: University of Colorado Herbarium (Boulder) and Grand Mesa, Uncompahgre, and Gunnison National Forests.

We require two Botany Technicians. These volunteers will look through rare plant herbarium specimens in the University of Colorado Herbarium (Boulder) and map known rare plant locations and absence locations on topographic maps for Grand Mesa, Uncompahgre, and Gunnison National Forests. They will search for rare plants throughout the Gunnison National Forest. Applicants must have their own vehicle (preferably four-wheel drive). You must also have the ability to use plant keys and identify plant species.

Gunnison Ranger District

Agency: U.S. Department of Agriculture Forest Service
Season: Summer
Contact: Robert Vermillion
216 N. Colorado
Gunnison, CO 81230
E-mail: rvermillion@fs.fed.us
Phone: (970) 641–0471

Description/Positions Available: The forest is located in southwestern Colorado. Gunnison is a small college town with excellent outdoor recreational opportunities.

We offer a Timber Management Program position. It is an opportunity to gain a variety of experience working on projects which may include completing a vegetation inventory, hazard tree risk surveys in campgrounds, reforestation surveys, GPS work, timber cruising/marking, and timber stand improvement. We have enough flexibility in the program to try and fit the needs of the individual to the available project work.

Medicine Bow–Routt National Forest, Yampa District

Agency: U.S. Department of Agriculture Forest Service
Season: Summer
Contact: Beth Redmond
P.O. Box 7
Yampa, CO 80483

E-mail: bredmond@fs.fed.us
Web: www.fs.fed.us/outernet/mrnf/
Phone: (970) 638–4516

Description/Positions Available: Located in Yampa, this 345,820-acre district manages the Gore Range and Flat Tops Mountains, which include the Sarvis Creek and Flat Tops wilderness areas. The district also maintains nine developed campgrounds and 198 miles of trails, and is active in range, wildlife, and timber administration.

Positions are available between Memorial Day and Labor Day in the areas of wildlife, range (botany), timber, backcountry trail maintenance, developed recreation, and wilderness and visitor information services. In addition to sharing and gaining valuable experience, volunteers may be provided with housing, equipment, and a weekly subsistence.

National Park Service/Amtrak

Agency: National Park Service
Season: Summer
Contact: Trails & Rails Coordinator
35110 Hwy. 194 E.
La Junta, CO 81050-9523
E-mail: BEOL_Interpretation@nps.gov
Phone: (719) 384–2596

Description/Positions Available: See description under Nationwide listings in the front of this directory.

This program is presented on board Amtrak's "Southwest Chief" between La Junta, Colorado and Albuquerque, New Mexico. We offer opportunities for Trails & Rails volunteers to ride once a month between these two cities. There are no housing, camping or lodging facilities provided by the program. The only expenses covered are those associated with the actual program.

Rocky Mountain Arsenal National Wildlife Refuge

Agency: U.S.. Fish and Wildlife Service

Season: Year-round
Contact: Refuge Volunteer Coordinator
RMANWF U.S. Fish and Wildlife Service
Bldg. 111
Commerce City, CO 80022-1748
Web: www.pmrma.army.mil
Phone: (303) 289-0557

Description/Positions Available: We are seeking Roving Interpreters-Bikers or Hikers with a minimum age of sixteen. Your purpose is to expand the public's knowledge about land use and the environment. This involves walking or biking the Refuge's nature trails, offering direction and guidance to visitors, providing interpretation, and answering questions about the site, presenting accurate up-to-date information about the Refuge, its history, natural resources and cleanup, and the completion of required reporting forms. Helpful applicant qualifications include a background in natural science, the ability to speak clearly and accurately, comfort in dealing with the public and approaching strangers, leadership and group management skills, enthusiasm about/ interest in the Refuge. You will report to an outdoor recreation specialist and participate in informal feedback and review sessions. There will be formal written feedback and review session with a supervisor once a year. You will receive the following training: seven hours of orientation yearly, three hours of Health and Safety/Cleanup (during quarterly volunteer meetings), eight hours of CPR and first aid, one hour of Roving Interpreter Operations. You are expected to spend four hours/month on the trails, attend monthly volunteer meetings, meet as needed with all Roving Interpreters and attend scheduled meetings with a supervisor. Your work will take you to various trails on Rocky Mountain Arsenal. This position provides the opportunity to expand your knowledge of natural science and to use creativity in interpretation. You can make a real difference in the public's understanding of the natural world through interaction with all ages and kinds of people. It is also a chance to discover and enjoy the many facets of the Refuge, and to purchase a

Refuge fishing permit at forty hours of service.

Rocky Mountain Arsenal National Wildlife Refuge

Agency: U.S. Fish and Wildlife Service
Season: Year-round
Contact: Volunteer Coordinator
RMANWF U.S. Fish and Wildlife Service
Bldg. 111
Commerce City, CO 80022-1748
Web: www.pmrma.army.mil
Phone: (303) 289-0557

Description/Positions Available: We need National Wildlife Refuge Tour Guides age eighteen or over. You will educate the public about environmental and land use issues. Your duties include guiding visitors on a tram tour of the Refuge including ensuring that visitors are registered and safely board and depart the tram. You will also present information from a prepared script about the Refuge and answer questions about the Refuge and its activities. You will manage the group during the duration of the tour and complete required reports in a timely fashion. Useful skills include the ability to speak easily and distinctly before an audience, enthusiasm, sense of humor, the ability to handle difficult situations with tact and courtesy, an interest in working with the public, and a background in natural science. You will be supervised through reports to a Park Ranger, in the Visitor Services section, as well as receiving formal feedback at review sessions. Informal feedback will be provided where appropriate. You will receive written feedback and review once a year from your supervisor and an evaluation by tour participants. You will be trained in several ways. This includes twelve hours of pre-service (seven hours Orientation; two hours Mammals; two hours Raptors; one hour Wildlife Health and BioMonitoring); eight hours of yearly CPR and first aid; four hours of Tour Guide Operations, and three hours of Health and Safety/Cleanup (during quarterly volunteer meetings). You must spend at least six hours preparing and must deliver two tours each month. You must also attend volunteer meetings, periodic meetings of all Refuge Tour Guides, and meetings with your supervisor. This position will allow you to help the public better understand the natural world and the human impact upon it. You will increase your knowledge of the environment and the natural habitat at the Refuge and view wildlife close to home. You will have the chance to improve your presentation skills through your own creativity and to network with professionals in the field of biology and wildlife management. You will be eligible to purchase a Refuge fishing permit after forty hours of service.

Royal Gorge Field Office, Bureau of Land Management

Agency: Bureau of Land Management
Season: Year-round
Contact: Diana Kossnar
3170 East Main St.
Canon City, CO 81212
E-mail: Diana_Kossnar@co.blm.gov
Web: www.co.blm.gov/ccdo/canon.htm

Description/Positions Available: The Shelf Road Recreation Area is located 8 miles north of Canon City, Colorado. The elevation is approximately 6,500 feet, and the weather is mild.

We need a Campground Host. The host oversees two small (twelve-unit) campgrounds at the Shelf Road Recreation Area. The area is a world renowned sport rock-climbing (limestone) site. The host's role is primarily to meet and greet campers, collect camping fees, and report any problems to the local Bureau of Land Management office. Other optional duties include general clean up around the campground and light trail maintenance. Annual visitation to the area is approximately 22,000.

Roxborough State Park

Agency: State parks
Season: Year-round
Contact: Heather Poe
4751 Roxborough Dr.
Littleton, CO 80125
E-mail: roxborough.park@state.co.us
Web: www.parks.state.co.us
Phone: (303) 973–3959

Description/Positions Available: Roxborough State Park is a beautiful natural area located just southwest of metro Denver. This park is nationally recognized for its scenic and natural values.

Roxborough is looking for groups and individuals to assist with habitat restoration projects, trail maintenance, and other maintenance projects. Volunteers are welcome to sign up for a one-time event or to make an ongoing commitment. Projects are generally scheduled between April and October. Special projects are planned for Earth Day (April 20th), National Trails Day (June 1), and Colorado Cares Day (July 27). Please contact the park directly for details. Roxborough State Park will recruit Volunteer Naturalists to lead school tours and public programs beginning in October 2002. The park offers extensive training and ongoing support. The initial training course is scheduled for February 2003.

San Juan Mountains Association

Agency: NON PRO
Season: Summer
Contact: Kathe Hayes, Volunteer Coordinator
P.O. Box 2261
Durango, CO 81301
E-mail: khayes@fs.fed.us
Web: www.sjma.org
Phone: (970) 385–1310

Description/Positions Available: The San Juan Mountains Association, created in 1988, is a nonprofit located in southwestern Colorado.

Our mission is to "enhance personal and community stewardship of natural, cultural and heritage resources on public and other lands in Southwest Colorado through interpretation, information, education and participation." We partner with land management agencies such as state parks, the U.S. Forest Service and the Bureau of Land Management.

SJMA has a variety of programs available for volunteers on public and other lands. These include positions as Wilderness Information Specialists, Ghost Riders, Arborglyphs Documenters, and Cultural Site Stewards. We also offer opportunities in the Chimney Rock Archeological Area and the Clean Forests Initiative as well as positions for those seeking an alternative Spring Break. In addition we coordinate trail projects and workdays on public lands. SJMA has bookstores located in Durango, Pagosa, and Dolores, Colorado.

Uncompahgre National Forest, Norwood Ranger District

Agency: U.S. Department of Agriculture Forest Service
Season: Summer
Contact: Kathy Peckham, Recreation Staff
P.O. Box 388
Norwood, CO 81423
E-mail: kpeckham@fs.fed.us
Web: www.fs.fed.us/r2/gmug/
Phone: (970) 327–4261

Description/Positions Available: Located in the heart of the San Juan Mountains, the Uncompahgre National Forest includes two wilderness areas and the beautiful Uncompahgre Plateau. More than 100 miles of hiking trails can be found in the area, from elevations starting as low as 7,000 feet and rising to as high as 14,000 feet. Near the historic mining town and modern-day ski resort of Telluride, recreation opportunities are unlimited. Telluride hosts music and art festivals each weekend throughout the summer months.

A Trail Crew Assistant is needed to assist with trail reconnaissance, trail maintenance, and sign installation (late May–June); the work will focus on hiking the area trails, recording obvious problems (e.g., fallen logs), and reporting back to the Forest Service. By mid-summer work shifts from this to assisting Forest Service personnel in conducting trail maintenance using crosscut saws and hand tools. Sign installation will be ongoing throughout the summer. The job also includes dayhiking with occasional overnight backpacking, a willingness to work independently, a moderate-to-high level of fitness, and a willingness to conduct sometimes strenuous trail maintenance work. Training, vehicle, and field supplies will be provided at the Bunkhouse accommodations near Telluride. Applicants must provide their own backpacking equipment, including tent and sleeping bag.

Vega State Park

Agency: State parks
Season: Summer
Contact: Chris Childs, Park Manager
P.O. Box 186
Collbran, CO 81624
E-mail: vega.park@state.co.us
Web: www.coloradoparks.org

Description/Positions Available: Located 54 miles east of Grand Junction, this park features a 900-acre reservoir nestled at 8,000 feet in alpine forests. The area is known for trout fishing, water sports, and spectacular scenery.

A Campground Host is needed to assist campers and provide information, ensure fee compliance, and perform routine cleaning and other light maintenance. Campsite and tools are provided. The campsite's facilities include water, electrical, and sewer hookup. Applicants committing to a minimum ten-week stay are preferred, as are those with previous experience. Positions generally work Memorial Day through Labor Day.

Volunteers for Outdoor Colorado

Agency: NON PRO
Season: Year-round
Contact: Leilani Fintus
600 S. Marion Pkwy.
Denver, CO 80210
E-mail: voc@voc.org
Web: www.voc.org

Description/Positions Available: We need volunteers for Outdoor Colorado's Clearinghouse statewide. Positions include anything from Web masters to backcountry fieldwork, research, and wildlife.

White River National Forest

Agency: U.S. Department of Agriculture Forest Service
Season: Summer
Contact: Joanne Lyon
806 W. Hallam
Aspen, CO 81611
E-mail: jlyon@fs.fed.us
Web: www.fs.fed.us/r2/whiteriver/
Phone: (970) 925–3445

Description/Positions Available: Aspen Ranger District is surrounded by the Maroon-Snowmass Wilderness, Hunter Fryingpan Wilderness and Collegiate Peaks Wilderness.

We offer posts providing visitor information at the Maroon Valley Entrance Station, as well as opportunities for Wilderness Rangers and Trail Crews. Housing is available for full time volunteers.

White River National Forest, Rifle Ranger District

Agency: U.S. Department of Agriculture Forest Service
Season: Summer
Contact: Patricia McGuire
0094 Country Rd. 244
Rifle, CO 81650

E-mail: pmcguire@fs.fed.us
Phone: (970) 625–2371

Description/Positions Available: Rifle, Colorado, is a small farming/ranching community on the western slope of Colorado. The Rifle Ranger District has an active recreation program. Other major workloads include range management, invasive plant species eradication, and wildlife biology.

We are looking for volunteers to work in recreation, range management, invasive plant species eradication, and wildlife biology.

Connecticut

Northwest Park and Nature Center

Agency: State parks
Season: Year-round
Contact: Kim Benton
145 Lang Rd.
Windsor, CT 06095
Web: www.northwestpark.org
Phone: (860) 285–1886

Description/Positions Available: We operate throughout 473 acres of diverse habitats including, fields, woodland swamps, a bog, a pond, and various types of forest environments in northern Connecticut. We have 15 miles of trails, an interpretative center, an animal barn, a maple sugar house, and a tobacco museum. Cross-country skiing and snowshoeing are offered during the winter months.

Volunteers can assist with animal care and feeding and help with ground and trail maintenance. Internships are available on a seasonal basis. Interns primarily assist the environmental educator with teaching school programs for ages three to twelve. Interns feed and care for captive indoor and barn animals. Assisting the naturalist with various environmental duties is also possible.

Delaware

Delaware State Parks

Agency: State parks
Season: Year-round
Contact: Volunteer Administrator
89 Kings Hwy.
Dover, DE 19901
E-mail: parkinfo@dnrec.state.de.us
Web: www.dnrec.state.de.us
Phone: (302) 739-3197

Description/Positions Available: Catch the spark! Volunteer at Delaware State Parks. Look for specific volunteer opportunities on our Web site or send us an e-mail.

Florida

Canaveral National Seashore

Agency: National Park Service
Season: Year-round
Contact: Laura Henning
308 Julia St.
Titusville, FL 32796
E-mail: maureen_picard@nps.gov
Web: www.nbbd.com or www.nps.gov/cana
Phone: (321) 267–1110

Description/Positions Available: Volunteers lead programs, assist with environmental education programs, and work at the visitor center, Seminole Rest, and/or Eldora House. They also help maintain trails, screen turtles, and do resource management. We only have one camping site, and that is committed for the next two years so no accommodations are provided.

Fanning Springs State Park

Agency: State parks
Season: Year-round
Contact: Rob Lacy
11650 NW 115th St.
Chiefland, FL 32626
E-mail: ppds@svic.net
Web: www.myflorida.com/communities/learn/stateparks/district2/fanningsprings/index.htm
Phone: (352) 493–6736

Description/Positions Available: Located on the banks of the beautiful and historic Suwannee River, this 191-acre park is an active person's dream. The park has a swimming area, picnic areas, boardwalks, a canoe camp, ball fields, nature trails, boating, and fishing docks.

Volunteers are needed to serve as Camp Hosts, Administrative Support, Maintenance and Construction Technicians, special event Planners and Officials, and Groundskeepers.

Florida State Parks

Agency: State parks
Season: Year-round
Contact: Phillip A. Werndli
3900 Commonwealth Blvd., Ms 535
Tallahassee, FL 32399
E-mail: volunteer@dep.state.fl.us
Web: www.dep.state.fl.us/parks/

Description/Positions Available: We are recruiting Campground Hosts, Resource Management Volunteers, Park Interpreters, Trail Building, and Maintenance staff. You may also contact any Florida state park directly about additional volunteer opportunities (more than 150 parks statewide).

Gulf Islands National Seashore

Agency: National Park Service
Season: Year-round
Contact: Dick Zani, Volunteer Coordinator
1801 Gulf Breeze Pkwy.
Gulf Breeze, FL 32563-5000
E-mail: Dick_Zani@nps.gov
Web: www.nps.gov/guis/

Description/Positions Available: We operate throughout the Florida District, which includes Fort Pickens Area, Fort Barrancas Area, Santa Rosa Area & Naval Live Oaks Area.

We are looking for Campground Hosts, an Interpretation and Visitor Center Assistant, a Cultural Resource Assistant, and a Maintenance Assistant.

Gulf Islands National Seashore

Agency: National Park Service
Season: Year-round
Contact: Dick Zani, Volunteer Coordinator
1801 Gulf Breeze Pkwy.
Gulf Breeze, FL 32563-5000

E-mail: Dick_Zani@nps.gov
Web: www.nps.gov/guis/

Description/Positions Available: We operate in the Mississippi District, which includes the Davis Bayou Area.

A Campground Host is required. We are also looking for Interpretation and Visitor Center Assistants.

Manatee Springs State Park

Agency: State parks
Season: Year-round
Contact: Rob Lacy
11650 NW 115th St.
Chiefland, FL 32626
E-mail: ppds@svic.net
Web: www.myflorida.com/communities/learn/stateparks/district2/manateesprings/index.htm
Phone: (352) 493–6736

Description/Positions Available: This pristine 2,373-acre park is located along the banks of the historic Suwannee River. It is made up of one of the largest first-magnitude springs in Florida, with a crystal clear creek running to the Suwannee River. Along with the aquatic ecosystems, cypress swamps, hardwood hammocks and high pine communities support a diverse population of flora and fauna.

Volunteers are needed to serve as Camp Hosts, help with reforestation projects, provide administrative support, park and trail maintenance on 8.5 miles of existing trail and more than 16 miles of proposed trails, Ranger Station Attendant, and special event Planners and Officials.

Nature Coast Trail State Park

Agency: State parks
Season: Year-round
Contact: Rob Lacy
11650 N.W. 115th St.
Chiefland, FL 32626
E-mail: ppds@svic.net
Web: www.myflorida.com/communities/learn/stateparks/district2/naturecoast/index.htm

Phone: (352) 493–6736

Description/Positions Available: This 32-mile-long multiple-use trail traverses a historic railbed through beautiful north Florida farm lands and quaint small towns and has access to state parks and other natural areas.

Volunteers are needed to maintain and patrol the trail, plan and officiate special events, and assist trail users. Benefits include free camping.

Ocala National Forest, Lake George Ranger District

Agency: U.S. Department of Agriculture Forest Service
Season: Year-round
Contact: Bret Bush or Johnnie Pohlers
4255 N.E. 64 Ave. Rd.
Silver Springs, FL 34488
E-mail: bbush@fs.fed.us
Phone: (352) 625–2520

Description/Positions Available: Ocala National Forest is 383,000 scenic acres in central Florida. Between the river boundaries of this forest lie central highlands, coastal lowlands, swamps, springs, and hundreds of lakes and ponds. The mild winters attract many "snowbirds" to the numerous campgrounds on the Ocala. The Lake George Ranger District has an active year-round volunteer program. Volunteers are needed to serve as Campground Hosts. There is a lot of competition for winter positions. Those who can stay for a minimum of six months will be considered first. Summer positions are almost always available, and incentives are provided for those that stay in the hot months. Volunteers are also needed for trails maintenance, recreation maintenance, and visitor services.

Oscar Scherer State Park

Agency: State parks
Season: Year-round
Contact: Scott Spaulding
1843 S. Tamiami Trail

Osprey, FL 34229
E-mail: Scott.Spaulding@dep.state.fl.us
Web: www.myflorida.com

Oscar Scherer State Park is located in central West Florida. The park is minutes away from Gulf Beaches and local attractions. Oscar Scherer State Park is composed of 1,384 acres. Visitors can enjoy recreational opportunities such as swimming, fishing, canoeing, camping, picnicking, hiking, and nature study.

Trail Maintenance Volunteers and Exotic Plant Control Volunteers are needed in all seasons.

Panhandle Pioneer Settlement

Agency: NON PRO
Season: Year-round
Contact: Jan Rosenberg
P.O. Box 215
Blountstown, FL 32424
E-mail: twodivys@gtcom.net
Web: www.panhandlepioneer.org
Phone: (850) 674–6791

Description/Positions Available: The Panhandle Pioneer Settlement is a nonprofit organization dedicated to the preservation of rural Florida. The Settlement offers guests the opportunity to see Florida life as it was around the turn of the twentieth century. The community was founded in 1989 to document, research, and preserve folkways of past generations. In addition, it has acquired eleven period structures dating from 1840 to 1940.

We have year-round opportunities for maintenance and construction at the Settlement. We offer the following facilities/accommodations: two RV hookups or cabins with showers nearby. Please contact Jan Rosenberg at the number listed or Linda Smith at (850) 674–8055.

Timucuan Ecological & Historic Preserve

Agency: State parks
Season: Year-round

Contact: Paul Ghiotto, Volunteer Coordinator
13165 Mt. Pleasant Rd.
Jacksonville, FL 32225
Phone: (904) 641–7111

Description/Positions Available: We offer opportunities for Interpretation/Resource Management Volunteers. Your duties would include operating visitor information areas in the Ft. Caroline and Kingsley Plantation visitor centers and assisting as skills allow in designated outdoor projects. A background or cultivated interest in American history and/or natural history is desirable. Free dormitory housing is available at Kingsley and an RV/Camper concrete pad with full hookups is provided at Ft. Caroline for a married couple or individual. Volunteers work four consecutive 7.5-hour days each week. Time is allowed for grocery shopping and laundry chores. Assignment periods are generally Winter (Jan.-March), Spring (April-June), Summer (July-Sept.) and Fall (Oct.-Dec.).

Torreya State Park

Agency: State parks
Season: Year-round
Contact: Steve Cutshaw
HC 2 Box 70
Bristol, FL 32321
E-mail: torreya@nettally.com
Web: dep.state.fl.us
Phone: (850) 643–2674

Description/Positions Available: The high bluffs overlooking the Apalachicola River make Torreya State Park one of Florida's most scenic. Rising more than 150 feet above the river, the bluffs have been shaped and divided by deep ravines that have been eroded by streams throughout the centuries.

We offer the following posts: Campground Hosts, Store Keepers, Tour Guides, Nature Hike Guides, Interpreters, Trail Maintenance, and Maintenance Volunteers.

Georgia

Allatoona Lake

Agency: U.S Army Corps of Engineers
Season: Summer
Contact: Linda Hartsfield
P.O. Box 487
Cartersville, GA 30120
E-mail: linda.d.hartsfield@sam.usace.army.mil
Web: www.sam.usace.army.mil/op/rec/
allatoon/default.htm
Phone: (770) 382–4700

Description/Positions Available: The site is located in Cartersville, Georgia. It is approximately 35 miles northwest of Atlanta in an urbanized area.

Four couples at least twenty-one years of age or older are needed for two-day use areas (Riverside and Cooper's Furnace), located approximately 4 miles from Cartersville, GA. These two-day use areas have two shelters each and the park hosts will work four days on and four days off. A campsite with water, sewage, electricity and a restricted-use telephone are provided. Gates are to be opened at 8:00 A.M. and closed at 9:30 P.M. daily. Hosts will man the gatehouse on Saturdays, Sundays, and holidays for traffic control and visitor assistance and be within the park during the other days of the week if they are on their four-day work rotation. There are no fees to collect. Park Hosts will keep a calendar of shelter reservations, issue volleyballs and horseshoes to the shelter users, and post daily generation schedules on the bulletin board at the gatehouse. An air-conditioned gatehouse is provided. There are no cleaning responsibilities. There is a two-pet limit. No vicious pets are allowed. No one else other than the host couple can live in the RV. You will make patrols of the park and report any discrepancies to the Operation Manager's Office. Cooper's Furnace is less than a 1-mile round trip. Riverside is approximately a 1-mile round trip. Training will be provided. Park Hosts must provide their own factory-built, self-contained camper trailer, or motor home. Please contact us in December, January, or February.

Amicalola Falls State Park

Agency: State parks
Season: Year-round
Contact: Bob Bolz/Jennifer Pack
240 Amicalola Falls State Park Rd.
Dawsonville, GA 30534
E-mail: bob-bolz@mail.dnr.state.ga.us
Web: ngeorgia.com/parks/amicalola.html
Phone: (706) 265–4703

Description/Positions Available: The park is located in the North Georgia Mountains approximately 50 miles north of Atlanta. It contains several miles of trails, interpretive programming year-round, and visitor center services.

We offer flexible positions depending on volunteers' experience and availability. These may include Trail Maintenance, Programming, and/or Customer Relations.

Andersonville National Historic Site

Agency: National Park Service
Season: Year-round
Contact: Volunteer Coordinator
Rte. 1, Box 800
Andersonville, GA 31052
Phone: (229) 924–0343

Description/Positions Available: Andersonville National Historic Site is a memorial to all Americans held as prisoners of war. The 500-acre site includes an active National Cemetery, the site of Camp Sumter (Civil War era prison), and the National Prisoner of War Museum.

Volunteers are needed for a variety of projects including photography, data-entry, diary transcription, and general grounds maintenance. Housing is available.

Chattahoochee National Forest

Agency: U.S. Department of Agriculture Forest Service
Season: Year-round
Contact: Mike Davis
3941 Hwy. 76
Chatsworth, GA 30705
E-mail: madavis@fs.fed.us
Web: www.fs.fed.us/conf/welcome.htm

Description/Positions Available: The main focus of opportunities is the Cohutta Wilderness, Cohutta Ranger District, Chatsworth. This is a 37,000-acre wilderness located along the Georgia/Tennessee border approximately two hours north of Atlanta.

We need Trail Maintenance Volunteers throughout the year.

Chattahoochee-Oconee National Forests

Agency: U.S. Department of Agriculture Forest Service
Season: Summer
Contact: Luana W. Kitchens
1755 Cleveland Hwy.
Gainesville, GA 30501
E-mail: lkitchens@fs.fed.us
Web: www.fs.fed.us/conf/welcome.htm
Phone: (770) 297–3016

Description/Positions Available: The Chatta-hoochee National Forest is located in the Mountains of North Georgia, and the Oconee National Forest is located in middle Georgia. We have seven districts, Armuchee, Brasstown, Chattooga, Cohutta, Tallulah, Toccoa, and Oconee.

Campground Hosts are needed for these forests in the southernmost reaches of the Appalachian Mountains. The natural environment features scenic beauty, tumbling streams, tall trees, long vistas and settings for outdoor recreation of all kinds. No government housing is available. However, a few small trailers are used to house volunteers. Most host campsites have electrical hookups, water, telephone, and/or radios. In addition, Interpretation Host Volunteers are needed to help operate information systems and a sales outlet at the visitor center. A background in natural science, history, or sales is helpful. Volunteers are needed between April and October, with a minimum three-month commitment required. Housing is available.

Georgia State Parks and Historic Sites

Agency: State parks
Season: Year-round
Contact: Chuck Gregory
205 Butler St., Ste. 1352
Atlanta, GA 30334
E-mail: ChuckG@mail.dnr.state.ga.us
Web: www.gastateparks.org
Phone: (404) 656–6539

Description/Positions Available: Georgia State Parks has volunteer and Campground Host opportunities in all of its sixty state parks and historic sites. To request a volunteer information packet, please call or write the volunteer coordinator or visit our Web site.

Campground Hosts, maintenance, office and clerical, interpretation and outdoor education, environmental clean-up, botanical and species surveys.

Hawaii

Hawaii Volcanoes National Park

Agency: National Park Service
Season: Year-round
Contact: VIP Coordinator
P.O. Box 52
HI Volcanoes NP, HI 96718
E-mail: Andrea_Kaawaloa@nps.gov
Phone: (808) 985–6013

Description/Positions Available: Internationally honored as a World Heritage Site and Biosphere Reserve, the park features the world's most active volcano. A tropical rainforest supports a rich diversity of plants and birds, including many endangered species. Cultural sites include ancient Hawaiian heiau temple ruins and historical structures.

Volunteers are needed to address the area's many challenging resource-management problems, involving alien plants and mammals.

Idaho

Big Piney Ranger District, Bridger-Teton NF

Agency: U.S. Department of Agriculture Forest Service
Season: Summer
Contact: John Haugh
P.O. Box 218
Big Piney, ID 83113
E-mail: jhaugh@fs.fed.us

Description/Positions Available: Big Piney is an isolated rural area dominated by the Wyoming Range. A portion of the Gros Ventre Wilderness Area is in the district.

We need a Backcountry Ranger to perform wilderness and non-wilderness patrols and light to moderate trail maintenance. This may involve individual or group work. Stock use is dependent upon experience.

Clearwater National Forest

Agency: U.S. Department of Agriculture Forest Service
Season: Summer
Contact: Volunteer Coordinator
Personnel Management, North Idaho Personnel Zone, 12370 Hwy. 12
Orofino, ID 83544
E-mail: pmgmt/r1_clearwater@fs.fed.us.gov
Phone: (208) 476–8317

Description/Positions Available: The forest includes almost 1.8 million acres in country where Lewis and Clark encountered rugged beauty in 1805 and 1806. Deep canyons, high ridges, and fast, clear streams mark this land. For centuries, people used the high ridges as routes across the mountain. Earliest of all were the Nez Perce Indians, followed by fur traders and later by Wellington Bird and Major Truax, who tried to build a road across the area for local miners. Evidence of these early travelers still exists. The forest hosts twenty developed campgrounds, many dispersed camping areas, 1,500-plus miles of hiking trails, many rivers and streams for canoeing or rafting, excellent hunting and fishing opportunities.

Volunteers are needed for Trail Crews, Timber Crews, Maintenance Work and Caretaking for the campgrounds, work centers, administrative sites. Campground Hosting and many other volunteer opportunities are also available. For more information, please contact the Volunteer Coordinators for the districts listed below: Lochsa District, Rte. 1, Box 398, Kooskia, ID, Phone: (208) 926–4284; Powell Work Center, Lolo, MT, 58847, Phone: (208) 942–3311, Palouse District, 1700 Hwy 6, Potlatch, ID, Phone: (208) 875–1131; North Fork District, 12730 Hwy 12, Orfino, ID, Phone: (208) 476–4541; Supervisor's Office, 12730 Hwy. 12, Orfino, ID, Phone: (208) 476–4541.

Craters of the Moon National Monument

Agency: National Park Service
Season: Summer primarily
Contact: Doug Owen
P.O. Box 29
Arco, ID 83213
E-mail: doug_owen@nps.gov
Phone: (208) 527–3257

Description/Positions Available: Please call or e-mail for available volunteer opportunities.

Idaho Department of Parks and Recreation

Agency: State parks
Season: Year-round
Contact: Kathryn Hampton, Volunteer Coordinator
5657 Warm Springs Ave.
Boise, ID 83716
E-mail: khampton@idpr.state.id.us
Web: idahoparks.org
Phone: (208) 334–4180, extension 242

Description/Positions Available: Statewide.

You have got to see it to believe it! Idaho offers some of the country's most diverse landscapes, from high mountain lakes to gigantic desert sand dunes. Its twenty-six state park preserve areas of historic and cultural significance, rare and exciting recreation value, and unique natural resources. We need seasonal (paid and unpaid) employees, typically between May and September. Some avail-

able positions include: Campground Hosts, Bridge Builders, Trail Builders/Brushers, natural/cultural/historical Interpreters, Carpenters, Mechanics. We may provide free housing, a full-hookup RV site, special access to remote trails and campgrounds, and reimbursement of expenses.

Idaho Department of Parks and Recreation

Agency: State parks
Season: Summer
Contact: Kathryn Hampton, Volunteer Coordinator
5657 Warm Springs Ave.
Boise, ID 83716
E-mail: khampton@idpr.state.id.us
Web: idahoparks.org
Phone: (208) 334–4180, extension 242

Description/Positions Available: We operate around the Idaho City Area Non-Motorized Trail System.

Our current recruitment plans include Bridge Builders, Yurt Maintenance, Fire Wood Cutters, and Trail Brushing/Clearing.

Nez Perce National Forest, Clearwater District

Agency: U.S. Department of Agriculture Forest Service
Season: Summer
Contact: Volunteer Coordinator
Rte. 2, Box 475
Grangeville, ID 83530
Phone: (208) 983–1963

Description/Positions Available: A wide diversity of landforms and ecological systems exists throughout the Nez Perce. Due in large part to steep terrain and sharp elevation differences (1,000–9,000 feet), the variety in flora ranges from dense, moist cedar groves along the Selway River to hot, dry desert ecosystems along the Snake and Salmon Rivers. A variety of recreation opportunities exist including camping, hiking, backpacking, and pleasure driving. The Forest's 2.4 million acres remain accessible by 2,450 miles of trails or rugged cross-country travel.

Volunteers are needed for Trail Maintenance/Construction Work/Caretaking (for campgrounds, work centers, administrative sites). Positions for Campgrounds/Picnic Ground Hosts and a variety of other occupations are also available. For more information contact the Volunteer Coordinator for the districts listed below: Salmon River District, HC 01, Box 70, White Bird, ID 83554; Elk City/Red River District, P.O. Box 416, Elk City, ID 83525; Clearwater District, Route 2, Box 475, Grangeville, ID 83530; Moose Creek District, HCR 75, Box 91, Kooskia, ID 83539.

Nez Perce National Forest, Red River District

Agency: U.S. Department of Agriculture Forest Service
Season: Spring to early fall
Contact: Gary Loomis
P.O. Box 416
Elk City, ID 83525-0416
Phone: (208) 842–2245

Description/Positions Available: This district administers portions of the Frank Church–River of No Return and the Gospel Hump wilderness areas in central Idaho.

Trailcrew Members are needed to do trail maintenance and construction. Applicants should have good backpacking, tool and low-impact living skills. Housing, subsistence, and equipment are provided. Our season runs from early April until the first part of October. Wilderness Ranger Assistants are needed to backpack into wilderness areas, educate visitors in zero-impact camping techniques, naturalize campsites, and perform light trail maintenance duties. Applicants should have backpacking skills, an interest in wilderness management, the ability to work alone and a desire to communicate with the public. No housing is available. Campground Hosts will perform light maintenance; mow weeds; greet and inform the public of

fee-payment procedures; and clean restrooms. A campsite with water hookup facilities is provided.

Payette National Forest, Krassel Ranger District

Agency: U.S. Department of Agriculture Forest Service
Season: Summer
Contact: Jenni Blake or Patti Stieger
P.O. Box 1026
McCall, ID 83638
E-mail: jblake01@fs.fed.us or pstieger@fs.fed.us
Web: www.fs.fed.us/r4/payette/
multiday-hikes.html
Phone: (208) 634–0600

Description/Positions Available: This district encompasses nearly one million acres, with 1,000 miles of trail used by hikers, horse groups, bicyclists, motor bikers, and snow recreationists. Most of the district is remote and features diverse wildlife, with elevations ranging from 3,000 to 9,000 feet. The district also administers a portion of the Frank Church–River of No Return Wilderness in central Idaho. The Big Creek Station is located outside the wilderness area with road access, while the Chamberlain Station is located deep within the wilderness area.

Station Assistants are needed at the Big Creek and Chamberlain stations and should have some skills in maintenance and public contact and be in good physical condition. Duties include assisting in routine maintenance of facilities and contacting forest visitors regarding travel plans, regulations, and trail conditions. The Big Creek station volunteer may assist with routine road patrols; therefore a current driver's license and a good driving record are required. Housing, a stipend, and transportation to the duty station from McCall will be provided. Interested persons should contact the district prior to May 15. We are also recruiting a Trail Crew. This requires two people to perform light trail maintenance and clearing using hand tools. Most work is in designated or proposed wilderness. Applicants must be able to carry at least a sixty-five pound backpack. Crews use crosscut

Payette National Forest, McCall and New Meadows District

Agency: U.S. Department of Agriculture Forest Service
Season: Summer
Contact: Al Becker
P.O. Box 1026
McCall, ID 83638
E-mail: abecker/r4,payette@fs.fed.us
Web: www.fs.fed.us/r4/payette/multiday-hikes.html
Phone: (208) 634–0714

Description/Positions Available: These two districts contain more than 150 high-mountain lakes, 750 miles of trails, and large expanses of backcountry. The terrain is steep and rugged. All volunteers must have backcountry skills and packing ability and will be using zero-impact camping ethics. Some positions are located in the Frank Church–River of No Return Wilderness. Others will be deployed on the South Fork of the Salmon River drainage.

Several trail positions are open to the volunteer employees including backcountry Trail Crew, Wilderness Guard Station Attendants, Facility Maintenance, Public Contact, Dispersed Recreation Cleanup, Trail Maintenance, Revegetation and Ecological Restoration. All positions require backcountry skills. When not in the backcountry bunkhouse, lodging will be provided at the Krassel Work Center, and a subsistence allowance can be expected.

Salmon and Challis National Forests

Agency: U.S. Department of Agriculture Forest Service
Season: Summer
Contact: Volunteer Coordinator
RR 2, Box 600
Salmon, ID 83467
Phone: (208) 756–5100

Description/Positions Available: Bordered by the impressive crests of the Continental Divide on the east and the Frank Church–River of No Return Wilderness to the west, these forests cover more than 4.3 million acres. The positions listed below are needed for the Cobalt, Leadore, North Fork, and Salmon, Challis, Middle Fork, Lost River and Yankee Fork districts. Campground Hosts are required to work weekends between June and October (dates vary with campground). A Range Rider is also needed for a one-month minimum stay between July 1 and September 1. Work includes inspecting cattle allotments to check for occupancy, forage use, and wildlife occurrence. Applicants must have riding skills. We would prefer you to provide your own horse. Wildlife Technicians are needed from June 1 to August 15. Good physical conditioning and driving skills are prerequisites for this job. Wildlife experience is also preferred. Fisheries Technicians are needed between June 1 and September 30. Fisheries experience is preferred. Wilderness Rangers are needed from June 15 to September 1. Good physical conditioning is required. Forestry Technicians are needed between June 1 and August 15. A natural resource background is preferred. Groundskeepers/Maintenance Volunteers are needed from June 15 to September 30. Carpentry and plumbing skills are preferred. Guard Station Attendants are needed between June 15 and September 30. Lawn maintenance, light carpentry/plumbing skills are preferred. Range technicians are needed from June 1 until September 1 to assist with range-management duties. Trails Maintenance Volunteers are needed between June and September. Visitor Center Attendants are required from Memorial Day weekend to Labor Day, helping to conduct tours. This position requires good people skills. A subsistence allowance of $12 per diem per individual, mileage reimbursement, and housing will be provided if funds are available.

Illinois

National Park Service/Amtrak

Agency: National Park Service
Season: Summer
Contact: Trails & Rails Coordinator
15701 S. Independence Blvd.
Lockport, IL 60441
E-mail: Superintendent_ILMI@nps.gov
Phone: (815) 588–6040

Description/Positions Available: See description under Nationwide listings in the front of this directory.

This program is presented on board Amtrak's "Texas Eagle" between Chicago, Illinois and St. Louis, Missouri. We need Trails & Rails volunteers to ride once a month between these two cities. There are no housing, camping, or lodging facilities provided by the program. The only expenses covered are those associated with the actual program.

Indiana

Indiana Dunes National Lakeshore

Agency: National Park Service
Season: Year-round
Contact: Jean-Pierre Anderson
1100 N. Mineral Springs Rd.
Porter, IN 46304
E-mail: jean-pierre_anderson@nps.gov
Web: www.nps.gov/indu
Phone: (219) 926–7561, extension 240

Description/Positions Available: Located on the southern tip of Lake Michigan, the Indiana Dunes National Lakeshore preserves more than 15,000 acres of sand dunes, wetlands, forests, and prairies.

We encourage volunteers to assist with environmental education programs and various festivals or work on the visitor center information desk, animal room projects, and various resource management projects.

Lincoln Boyhood National Monument

Agency: National Park Service
Season: Summer
Contact: Superintendent
Lincoln City, IN 47552
Phone: (812) 937–4541

Description/Positions Available: This 200-acre wooded and landscaped park is the place to learn about Abraham Lincoln and his family, who lived here in a pioneer community from 1816 to 1830. Facilities include the Memorial Visitor Center, the grave of Nancy Hanks Lincoln (Abe's mother), and the Lincoln Living Historical Farm—an operating reproduction of the kind of farmstead where Abraham Lincoln grew up.

We need a Gardener to wear historic nineteenth-century costumes while assisting in the maintenance of Living Farm garden, flower beds and field crops. Must be able to lift thirty lbs. and learn about hand-gardening practices of the early nineteenth century. Also must possess good communication and writing skills.

Iowa

Camp Courageous of Iowa

Agency: NON PRO
Season: Year-round
Contact: Tom Shank
12007 190th St.
Monticello, IA 52310
E-mail: tshank@campcourageous.org
Web: campcourageous.org

Description/Positions Available: Monticello, Iowa, is halfway between Dubuque and Cedar Rapids, approximately thirty minutes from each city.

We are continually looking for volunteers and people to fill various essential staffing positions.

Iowa Department of Natural Resources, Yellow River State Forest

Agency: State parks
Season: Spring to fall
Contact: Bob Honeywell
729 State Forest Rd.
Harpers Ferry, IA 52146
Phone: (563) 586–2254

Description/Positions Available: This area features rugged terrain, limestone cliffs, and trout streams close to the Mississippi River.

Volunteers needed to serve as Visitor Center Host and assist with trail maintenance, signing, timber stand improvement and tree planting (spring only). Free camping is available. Workmen's compensation insurance is also provided.

Kansas

Fort Scott National Historic Site

Agency: National Park Service
Season: Year-round
Contact: Galen R. Ewing
P.O. Box 918
Fort Scott, KS 66701
E-mail: galen_ewing@nps.gov
Web: www.nps.gov/fosc
Phone: (620) 223–0310

Description/Positions Available: We are located in southeast Kansas 90 miles south of Kansas City and 60 miles north of Joplin, Missouri.

We currently have openings for Visitor Center Greeters, Living History Demonstrators, and Prairie Conservation Work.

Kansas Department of Wildlife and Parks

Agency: State parks
Season: Year-round
Contact: Personnel Office
512 SE 25th Ave.
Pratt, KS 67124
Phone: (620) 672–5911

Description/Positions Available: Interpretive Naturalists are needed mainly in state parks to provide public programming about the flora, fauna, and history of Kansas. Much of the programming takes place on weekends and in the evening. You may also be required to assist park and wildlife personnel in nature trail development and other work. Excellent written and verbal communication skills are essential. Park

Attendants are needed to assist regular park staff with visitors. Communication and human-relations skills are important. Maintenance and Repair Assistants are also required to work mainly in parks-grounds management, operat-

ing equipment and assisting with facility development. Human-relations skills are important for these posts. We are recruiting Wildlife/ Fisheries Biologist Aides to work on several projects.

Kentucky

Abraham Lincoln Birthplace NHS

Agency: National Park Service
Season: Year-round
Contact: Patti Reynolds
2995 Lincoln Farm Rd.
Hodgenville, KY 42748
E-mail: Patti_Reynolds@nps.gov
Web: www.nps.gov/abli
Phone: (270) 358–3137

Description/Positions Available: Three miles south of Hodgenville, Kentucky on U.S. Hwy. 31E and Kentucky Hwy. 61.

Interpreters are needed to greet the public, give information and directions, sell publications, run audiovisual programs and discuss Lincoln's life. Trail Maintenance workers are also needed to maintain the park trails.

Cumberland Gap National Historical Park

Agency: National Park Service
Season: Year-round
Contact: Janice S Miracle
P.O. Box 1848
Middleboro, KY 40965
E-mail: Janice_miracle@nps.gov
Web: www.nps.gov/cuga
Phone: (606) 248–2817

Description/Positions Available: Located where the borders of Tennessee, Kentucky, and Virginia meet, Cumberland Gap forms a major break in the formidable Appalachian Mountain chain.

The Gap was the first and best route into the unknown land of Kentucky.

At least one position is needed for each of the following: Wilderness Road Campground Host; Visitor Center Receptionist; Hensley Settlement Host; Library Assistant; Cudjo Cave Guide; and Hensley Settlement Guide.

Daniel Boone National Forest

Agency: U.S. Department of Agriculture Forest Service
Season: Year-round
Contact: Laurie Smith
P.O. Box 429
Whitley City, KY 42653
E-mail: lauriesmith@fs.fed.us
Web: www.southernregion.fs.fed.us/boone/

Description/Positions Available: Stearns Ranger District, Whitley City, Kentucky.

We are looking for Trail Reconstruction Workers to oversee the repair of trails damaged by storms, mainly involving the clearing of uprooted trees. This will also include trail maintenance: brushing and placing reassurance markers.

Daniel Boone National Forest/Red River Gorge

Agency: U.S. Department of Agriculture Forest Service
Season: Year-round
Contact: Red River Gorge Trail Crew, Aimee Bell
705 W. College Ave.
Stanton, KY 40380
E-mail: trail_blazer1@juno.com

Description/Positions Available: We operate from the Stanton Ranger District/Red River Gorge, near Stanton.

We are looking for volunteers to do trail work and will provide them with training! We reroute trails, clear trails, put in steps for river access—basically anything the area needs.

Nashville District, U.S. Army Corps Of Engineers

Agency: U.S. Army Corps of Engineers
Season: Year-round

Contact: Volunteer Clearinghouse
P.O. Box 1070
Nashville, TN 37202
E-mail: Gayla.Mitchell@lrn02.usace.army.mil
Web: www.orn.usace.army.mil/volunteer
Phone: (800) 865–8337

Description/Positions Available: The Nashville District features ten beautiful lakes in Kentucky and Tennessee with numerous parks and campgrounds.

The area needs a Campground or Park Host, Visitor Center staff, Park or Trail Maintenance workers, Shoreline cleanup staff, Office Assistants and Fish and Wildlife Restorers. A free campsite is often provided.

Louisiana

Kisatchie National Forest, Calcasieu District

Agency: U.S. Department of Agriculture Forest Service
Season: Year-round
Contact: Glenn Coleman
Evangeline Ranger District, 9912 Hwy. 28
Boyce, LA 71409-9644
Phone: (318) 793–9427

Description/Positions Available: Kincaid Recreation Area offers swimming, fishing, and hiking in a relatively undisturbed natural setting. Secluded campgrounds feature modern facilities, electricity, and paved spurs. Valentine Lake offers additional recreation experiences and a campground overlooking the lake.

A Campground Host is needed to answer questions, help campers get settled, explain campground regulations, suggest things to do in the area, perform minor maintenance, and manage restrooms and bath-houses. In addition, we are looking to recruit a Recreation Host for interpretive services, light general maintenance, and bulletin board maintenance. Benefits include a free

campsite with water and electricity and a gray water dump.

Natchitoches National Fish Hatchery

Agency: U.S. Fish and Wildlife Service
Season: Year-round
Contact: Karen Kilpatrick, Hatchery Manager
615 Hwy. #1 S.
Natchitoches, LA 71457
E-mail: Karen_Kilpatrick@fws.gov
Web: natchitoches.fws.gov/
Phone: (318) 352–5324

Description/Positions Available: This hatchery is located in western central Louisiana, in historic Natchitoches, the oldest city in the Louisiana Purchase. Hatchery property is approximately 98 acres. It includes fifty-three man-made ponds, three in-pond raceways, and several buildings used for fish culture and facility maintenance. It also has a sixteen-tank, 9,000-gallon Public Aquarium that displays native fish and reptiles and an environmental education classroom with wet labs to accommodate thirty-two students. The hatchery employs a full-time staff of six people and occasionally recruits volunteers to help with special projects or busy seasons. Spring is the time when fish production is in full swing. Public environmental education programs occur throughout the year.

The positions needed will vary with season and workload but may include: assisting with hatching, rearing, and distribution of fish; helping complete facility maintenance projects; helping with public use programs; or maintenance in the environmental education classroom or public aquarium. Inquire with the hatchery manager if you are interested.

National Park Service/Amtrak

Agency: National Park Service
Season: Year-round
Contact: Trails & Rails Coordinator
419 Rue Decatur
New Orleans, LA 70130-1142
E-mail: Dusty_Warner@nps.gov
Phone: (504) 281–0511, extension 11

Description/Positions Available: See description under Nationwide listings in the front of this directory.

This program is presented on board Amtrak's "Sunset Limited" between New Orleans, Louisiana and Houston, Texas. We need Trails & Rails volunteers to ride once a month between these three cities. There are no housing, camping or lodging facilities provided by the program. The only expenses covered are those associated with the actual program.

Tensas River National Wildlife Refuge

Agency: U.S. Fish and Wildlife Service
Season: Year-round
Contact: Ava Kahn or Maury Bedford
2312 Fred Morgan, Sr. Rd.
Tallulah, LA 71282
E-mail: ava_kahn@fws.gov
Web: www.fws.gov/r4eao
Phone: (318) 575–2664

Description/Positions Available: We are located in northeast Louisiana approximately 15 miles southwest of Tallulah, which was the last documented home of the ivory-billed woodpecker and is home to the threatened Louisiana black bear. The refuge contains approximately 66,000 acres of bottomland hardwood forest and oxbow lakes, which once covered twenty-five million acres of the Mississippi Valley. Recreational/public use opportunities include: hunting, fishing, boating, nature/hiking trails, wildlife observation, photography, educational programs, autotour route.

Numerous possible volunteer opportunities are available including staffing a visitor center, manning hunter check stations during deer harvest, conducting or assisting with a variety of interpretive and/or environmental education programs. Seasonal opportunities may involve biological surveys and studies such as bird counts, banding, and/or monitoring, vegetation surveys, black bear tracking, trapping, and/or monitoring, reforestation, and trail maintenance.

Maine

Rachel Carson National Wildlife Refuge

Agency: U.S. Fish and Wildlife Service
Season: Summer
Contact: Volunteer Coordinator
321 Port Rd.
Wells, ME 04090
E-mail: FW5RW_RCNWR@FWS.GOV
Phone: (207) 646–9226

Description/Positions Available: The Rachel Carson National Wildlife Refuge protects salt marshes from Cape Elizabeth to Kittery, Maine. The refuge, now more than 5,000 acres, provides critical migration and wintering habitat for waterfowl and other migratory birds. More than 300 species of birds, mammals, reptiles, and amphibians may be seen on or from the refuge. The "Carson Trail" is located at the refuge headquarters on Route 9 in Wells. It is a 1-mile, accessible, self-guided path through pine-woods that affords beautiful views of the Little River estuary.

We offer diverse opportunities for local residents and long-term visitors to southern, coastal Maine. Volunteers may lead trail walks, maintain our 1-mile trail, conduct wildlife and/or plant surveys, etc. Please call prior to your visit to determine the availability of projects.

SERVE/Maine

Agency: State parks
Season: Year-round
Contact: Brenda Webber, Recruitment and Outreach Assistant
124 State House Station
Augusta, ME 04333
E-mail: corps.conservation@state.me.us
Phone: (207) 287–4931

Description/Positions Available: Volunteers are needed throughout the state for Environmental Education, Water Quality Monitoring, Graphic Design, Administrative Assistance, Public Relations, Data Entry, Legal Assistance, Fund-Raising, Backcountry Campsite Maintenance, Environmental Interpretation, Backcountry Trail-Building, and general Maintenance, as well as other fields.

Sunkhaze Meadows National Wildlife Refuge

Agency: U.S. Fish and Wildlife Service
Season: Summer
Contact: Tom Comish
1033 S. Main St.
Old Town, ME 04468
E-mail: Tom_Comish@fws.gov
Phone: (207) 827–6138

Description/Positions Available: We have opportunities for those willing to assist refuge staff in conducting the biological, public use, and maintenance programs on the refuge and satellite areas. Specific duties include wildlife surveys, development of species lists, trail construction and maintenance, boundary posting, and routine maintenance of refuge facilities and equipment. Volunteers can also assist in the development of public use facilities including interpretive exhibits, signs, and kiosks. The entering of data into computer programs and some writing will be required. The majority of the work will be in the field. Sunkhaze Meadows protects one of the largest peat bogs in Maine. The refuge is located 14 miles north of Bangor. It is semi-remote with few public facilities. Visitation is about 2,800 per year.

Two positions are needed, which are called Volunteer/Public Use Internships. A stipend of $125 per week will be offered, which may be increased to $150 per week if the budget allows.

The length of the assignment will be forty hours per week, up to fifteen weeks, beginning in late May or early June. Housing in a rustic cabin on Sunkhaze Stream is included. To apply, submit a resume with three references and a cover letter to Tom Comish at the address above. Selection will be made in early March.

Maryland

Assateague Island National Seashore

Agency: National Park Service
Season: Summer
Contact: Liz Davis
7206 National Seashore Lane
Berlin, MD 21811
E-mail: liz_davis@nps.gov
Web: www.nps.gov/asis/
Phone: (410) 641–1441

Description/Positions Available: Assateague Island is a 37-mile-long barrier island located off the Atlantic Coast. The island extends into two states, Maryland and Virginia. We feature pristine beaches, great birding opportunities and the famous wild horses.

Internship/Volunteer positions are available in several areas. Opportunities are limited for positions in which we provide living quarters, and supervisors screen applications to identify those who we hope will be the most valuable employees. Depending on the time of year, three park divisions host individuals who are placed through the Student Conservation Association (SCA). Applicants do not necessarily have to be college students. Some of these twelve-week positions are in summer but a few are in spring or autumn. The application process with the SCA is lengthy but could increase your chances for positions across the country. In addition to quarters and subsistence benefits, the SCA provides a travel grant to and from the park. Most of the college students working here as volunteer interns have been placed through our own Volunteer-in-the-Parks program, rather than SCA. All students need

to do to apply is send a letter of interest which indicates availability, a resume, a college transcript (need not be official), and two written references (one of which should be an employer or supervisor), may arrive under separate cover. Apply early! We provide free quarters for resident volunteer student interns or SCA volunteers. Volunteer student interns receive a subsistence allowance for food of $12 per diem.

Catoctin Mountain Park

Agency: National Park Service
Season: Year-round
Contact: Chief Ranger
6602 Foxville Rd.
Thurmont, MD 21788
E-mail: roger_steintl@nps.gov
Web: www.nps.gov/cato/
Phone: (301) 663–9330

Description/Positions Available: Featuring 6,000 heavily forested acres in the Blue Ridge Mountains of central Maryland, this park offers a rich variety of flora, fauna, and cultural history. Visitors can enjoy many recreational opportunities such as hiking, camping, and fishing.

Campground Hosts are needed and must be available for a four-week stay or longer, working thirty-five hours per week. A small subsistence may be provided. Hosts are responsible for greeting campers, providing information about the area, performing minor campsite clean up, and are available to campers for contacting a Ranger in emergencies. Owens Creek has hookups, but volunteers need to supply their own RV/camper. The central bathhouse has hot and cold water and showers. Misty Mount is a historic log cabin camp and features cabin housing with electric utilities and water. The camp also contains a swimming pool. Camp Round Meadow is a year-round camp with four modern dorms, a large gym, and other facilities. Trailer and utilities are provided, or we will give you access to a trailer pad with W/E/S hookups. We are also recruiting Trail Trustees to oversee more than 25 miles of wooded mountain trails. There are many positions available for those offering helping hands and strong backs, to help revitalize the trail system. Tools and instruction will be provided.

Chesapeake and Ohio Canal National Historic Park

Agency: National Park Service
Season: Year-round
Contact: John Noel
P.O. Box 4
Sharpsburg, MD 21782
E-mail: john_noel@nps.gov
Web: www.nps.gov/choh/co_vol.htm
Phone: (301) 714–2238

Description/Positions Available: The park is 184 miles long and parallels the Potomac River from Washington, D.C. to Cumberland, Maryland. The park preserves the history and ecology of the canal and towpath that was operational from 1850 to 1924. The towpath is a popular hiking/cycling route. We have a variety of trail maintenance opportunities for our towpath and connector trails. In addition, we have seven visitor centers and two living history canal boat programs that provide interpretive information and programs to the public.

The following positions are available: Trail Maintenance Worker, Staffing at front desks in visitor centers, Living history Interpreter on canal boat wearing 1870s period clothing, general maintenance work, Special Event Assistance throughout the year. We also offer opportunities for Bike Patrol members to ride the towpath and assist visitors, Office Assistance to the volunteer coordinator, and a Computer Technician familiar with basic computer skills.

Eastern Neck National Wildlife Refuge

Agency: U.S. Fish and Wildlife Service
Season: Year-round
Contact: Susan Talbott
1730 Eastern Neck Rd.
Rock Hall, MD 21661
E-mail: Susan_Talbott@fws.gov
Web: easternneck.fws.gov

Description/Positions Available: Eastern Neck National Wildlife Refuge is a 2,285-acre island located near the town of Rock Hall on Maryland's rural eastern shore, at the confluence of the Chester River and the Chesapeake Bay. The primary purpose of the refuge is the protection and management of habitat for migrating and wintering waterfowl, as well as the endangered Delmarva fox squirrel and the threatened bald eagle. In addition, Eastern Neck NWR provides the public with opportunities for wildlife-dependent outdoor recreation, such as hunting, fishing, environmental education, hiking, nature observation, and photography.

Be one of our Environmental Educators! School classes and youth groups visiting Eastern Neck National Wildlife Refuge need to be assured of an exciting educational program, but we are limited by the amount of staff and volunteer assistance we have available. If you would like the joy of teaching children about wildlife and conservation, this opportunity is for you. Enthusiasm for working with children is a must; previous experience teaching or working with children is useful, but not required. Most programs are held periodically during fall, spring, and summer, usually on weekdays. We are also hiring Biological Survey Assistants: so many species, so little time! Eastern Neck National Wildlife Refuge staff can't possibly complete all necessary biological surveys without the help of talented volunteers. If you have an interest and/or experience in wildlife monitoring, this opportunity is for you. Current monitoring efforts include waterfowl, songbirds, and an annual deer census. Wildlife identification skills would be very useful but not necessarily required if the desire to learn is strong. Time requirements vary throughout the year. We also need Outdoor Maintenance Assistants: There's a lot of upkeep required on a dynamic 2,300-acre National Wildlife Refuge like Eastern Neck! Enjoy working outdoors? Volunteers are responsible for trail maintenance, sign construction, vehicle maintenance, and more. Experience with general maintenance, hand and power tools, and carpentry is helpful. A regular time commitment is preferred, but we are flexible. Interpretation Specialist/ Naturalist: The public would like more opportunities to learn about the wildlife and management activities at Eastern Neck National Wildlife Refuge. We are looking for talented volunteers to develop interpretive programs, such as bird walks and trail hikes, as well as interpretive signs and written materials. Creativity and enthusiasm, along with a desire to expand and share your knowledge about wildlife, are the only requirements.

Fort McHenry National Monument and Historic Shrine

Agency: National Park Service
Season: Year-round
Contact: Vince Vaise
East Fort Ave.
Baltimore, MD 21230
E-mail: vince_vaise@nps.gov
Phone: (410) 962–4290, extension 236

Description/Positions Available: This park, located in south Baltimore, is the birthplace of "The Star Spangled Banner."

Interpreters are needed to present living-history programs illustrating soldier life during the War of 1812. Volunteers are also required to staff the information desk, give historical talks, care for the extensive museum collections, and perform maintenance duties. All uniforms and equipment are provided by the park.

Maryland State Parks

Agency: State parks
Season: Year-round
Contact: Helene Tenner
580 Taylor Ave., E-3
Annapolis, MD 21401
E-mail: Htenner@dnr.state.md.us
Web: www.dnr.state.md.us/publiclands/
Phone: (410) 260–8161

Description/Positions Available: We coordinate opportunities in forty-seven state parks located throughout the state, from the Atlantic coast to the Appalachian Mountains.

In summer Camp Hosts are especially in demand. Throughout the year volunteers can help with trail maintenance, interpretive programs, the Volunteer Ranger program, or Friends groups.

Massachusetts

Appalachian Mountain Club, Berkshire Trails Program

Agency: NON PRO
Season: Summer
Contact: Regional Trails Coordinator
150 North St., Suite 22
Pittsfield, MA 01201
Web: www.outdoors.org
Phone: (413) 443–0011

Description/Positions Available: A Volunteer Trail Crew is needed in the summer for unique weekly work on a variety of projects. Room and board, leaders, tools and training are all provided. The following positions are seasonal. We need two Trail Crew Leaders: you will work on Mt. Greylock State Reservation trails and the Appalachian Trail throughout western Massachusetts. You will be responsible for training and leading a volunteer crew of up to eight people per week in trail maintenance projects. This work will include construction of rock staircases and waterbars, building bridges, and general brushing and clearing. The leaders and crew are based out of various campsites throughout the Berkshire region in western Massachusetts. Crew Leaders must be able to work effectively with volunteers, possess good communications skills, self-motivation and the ability to motivate others. Desire to do hard work in the outdoors is vital. Experience in trail maintenance techniques is desirable. These posts relate to the summer and are paid $275 per week plus room and board. We also need four Appalachian Trail Ridgerunners. This job entails patrolling the Appalachian Trail in Connecticut and southern Massachusetts from early June until Labor Day. Responsibilities include educating hikers about local trail rules and regulations; offering assistance to hikers; tracking use data; reporting conditions; and generally being a presence on the AT. Shifts are generally ten days on, four days off. Must have experience backpacking and be comfortable in the woods for ten days at a time (not a wilderness setting). Experience with the public is preferred. Benefits include $255 per week, a local cabin where volunteers can stay on days off and store their belongings, and free AMC membership (valid June 4–August 31). We are also looking for a Program Assistant. You would play an integral part in the Berkshires Trails Program by working with the Regional Trails Coordinator on a range of activities that support the Volunteer Trail Crew and the Ridgerunner programs in particular. This position is indoors and outdoors and everything in between. The post gives you the opportunity to become engaged in many aspects of trail management, including logistical assistance, reporting, information dissemination, and trail maintenance. Computer skills are preferred. For more information please visit our Web site or give us a call.

Minute Man National Historic Park

Agency: Minute Man National Historical Park
Season: Year-round
Contact: Volunteer Coordinator
174 Liberty St.
Concord, MA 01742
E-mail: mima_info@nps.gov
Web: www.nps.gov/mima
Phone: (978) 369–6993

Description/Positions Available: Minute Man NHP is located 16 miles outside Boston, in the suburban towns of Lexington, Lincoln, and Concord, Massachusetts. Consisting of approximately 1,200 acres, Minute Man protects, preserves and interprets the opening battles of the American Revolution (April 18–19, 1775) through its historic sites, structures, and landscapes. It is also a center for the study of the nineteenth-century American Literary Renaissance. The park is located off I–95/Route 128 (exit 30B).

We are looking for Trail Workers, Naturalists, and Historical Interpreters to help us in the maintenance of the environment and the dissemination of information on the cultural legacy preserved here.

Michigan

Hiawatha National Forest, Munising Ranger District

Agency: U.S. Department of Agriculture Forest Service
Season: Summer
Contact: Janel Crooks
400 East Munising Ave.
Munising, MI 49862
E-mail: jmcrooks@fs.fed.us
Phone: (906) 387–2512, extension 25

Description/Positions Available: Located in the wilds of Michigan's Upper Peninsula, the Hiawatha National Forest encompasses almost a million acres of land. On the Munising Ranger District, that land includes Grand Island National Recreation Area, two wildernesses, several semi-primitive areas, and a plentitude of recreational opportunities including fabulous mountain biking, hiking, and cross-country ski trails. The town of Munising, nestled below the hills beside Lake Superior, is a full-service community of about 3,000 people. Within 40 miles lies the city of Marquette, a university town with complete shopping and regional medical centers.

If this setting appeals to you, and if you have strengths in visitor service, you may be just the volunteer we need! During the summer season (May/June–September), our interagency (U.S. Forest Service/National Park Service) visitor center is a busy place! Visitors come seeking information and permits when planning trips into the National Forest and Pictured Rocks National Lakeshore. Duties include answering phones, talking with visitors, and selling permits and sales items. Skills in photography could also be very helpful, and naturalist/interpreter skills are always welcome! We'll consider applications from couples and/or individuals. Resumes should include descriptions of relevant experience and at least five references. Send resumes via e-mail, postal mail, or give us a call.

Isle Royale National Park

Agency: National Park Service
Season: Summer
Contact: Liz Valencia
800 E. Lakeshore Dr.
Houghton, MI 49931
E-mail: liz_valencia@nps.gov
Web: www.nps.gov/isro
Phone: (906) 487–7153

Description/Positions Available: Isle Royale National Park is a wilderness archipelago surrounded by Lake Superior. The island features rugged ridge and valley topography in northern hardwoods and boreal forests with numerous interior lakes and swamp and the spectacular scenery of Lake Superior. The island is home to 165 miles of maintained hiking trails. Fishing, backpacking, boating, canoeing, and kayaking are also popular activities.

Volunteers are needed for summer-long (June–August) positions, including Librarian/Resource Center, Photography/Cultural Resources, Campground Host, Natural Resources, Trail and Campground Maintenance, Ship Purser, Interpreter/Visitor Center, and Backcountry Ranger. Dormitory housing is provided for most positions, as is a daily food stipend and complimentary passage to the island on the RANGER III vessel. Applications are available on the park Web site and are due by March 15.

Jordan River National Fish Hatchery

Agency: U.S. Fish and Wildlife Service
Season: Year-round
Contact: Rick Westerhof
6623 Turner Rd.
Elmira, MI 49730
E-mail: rick_westerhof@fws.gov
Phone: (231) 584–2461

Description/Positions Available: The Jordan River National Fish Hatchery is located in the northern portion of the lower peninsula of Michigan. The hatchery is in the Jordan River Valley, on the Jordan River—a designated Wild and Scenic River. Volunteers can assist hatchery staff in many aspects of their duties, including: fish culture activities involving raising/releasing lake trout for the Great Lakes, public outreach, facilities maintenance, and landscaping.

We are in the process of organizing a "Friends Group" for the hatchery. Volunteers are needed to assist in this effort and to handle public outreach duties by meeting/greeting the public and giving tours. Volunteers can also assist in fish culture activities such as feeding fish, cleaning tanks, and raceways, sample counting, etc.

Ottawa National Forest

Agency: U. S. Department of Agriculture Forest Service
Season: Summer
Contact: Jeanmarie Hagan
Hwy. M-28 E.
Kenton, MI 49965
E-mail: jhagan@fs.fed.us
Phone: (906) 852–3500

Description/Positions Available: Our campgrounds range from eighteen to twenty-seven sites, have rustic facilities, and require self-contained camping units. No electricity is provided, but water is available at hand pumps. We operate from May 15 to October 15. The fishing and boating are excellent!

To assist in the administration of our sites we intend to recruit Campground Hosts for three beautiful lakefront campgrounds. Hosts who can be available approximately 40 hours a week to make visitor contacts and perform light maintenance are needed. If you are interested, please call the number above. A stipend for LP gas is available. The minimum length that you can be employed with us is thirty days. The sites at Lake St. Kathryn, Parch Lake, and Norway Lake are still available.

Ottawa National Forest, Kenton Ranger District

Agency: U.S. Department of Agriculture Forest Service
Season: Summer
Contact: Steve Babler
Iron River District, 990 Lalley Rd.
Iron River, MI 49935
E-mail: sbabler@fs.fed.us
Phone: (906) 265–5139

Description/Positions Available: A Breeding Bird Census is taken at 103 plots across the Ottawa National Forest in a variety of different habitat types. This project will take place between June 7 and 9, 2002, (Friday night, Saturday, and Sunday morning). Housing is provided at beautiful Camp Nesbit, located on Nesbit Lake in the Western Upper Peninsula of Michigan. There are bunkhouses with separate showers and bathroom facilities available at the camp. Campgrounds are also available in the area. Meals are provided, starting with snacks on Friday afternoon and culminating with Sunday lunch. Volunteers are encouraged to bring their own binoculars, field clothing, and hiking boots. Bird song field guides and tapes are helpful but optional.

Volunteer should have the ability to identify birds by sound. Intermediate and expert birders are desirable, but beginners are welcome. You must be able to do moderate-to-easy hiking.

Ottawa National Forest, Ontonagon District

Agency: U.S. Department of Agriculture Forest Service
Season: Summer
Contact: Dawn Buss
1209 Rockland Rd.
Ontonagon, MI 49953
Phone: (906) 884–2411

Description/Positions Available: Located in the western Upper Peninsula of Michigan, the area's northern hardwood forests, lakes and streams support a wide variety of fish, wildlife and recreation opportunities.

Opportunities exist for volunteers to write interpretive text for 1.7 miles of trail; serve as a Campground Host; and maintain the North Country National Scenic Trail. Training, tools, and a free campsite will be provided, but volunteers must bring their own camping gear.

Pictured Rocks National Lakeshore

Agency: National Park Service
Season: Summer
Contact: Gregg Bruff
P.O. Box 40
Munising, MI 49862
E-mail: gregg_bruff@nps.gov
Web: nps.gov/piro
Phone: (906) 387–2607

Description/Positions Available: Towering cliffs, eastern hardwood forest, inland lakes, Twelve Mile Beach, shipwrecks, and the Au Sable Light Station are a few of the attractions of the park on Lake Superior. The Lakeshore stretches some 42 miles along the shoreline but is only 5 miles wide at its widest point.

Spend a summer in Michigan's great north woods. Volunteers assist Lakeshore staff in numerous ways including Campground Hosting, Au Sable Light Station Tour Guides, Visitor Center Assistants, Natural Resource Research Assistants, Backcountry Ranger Patrol, and in trails maintenance. Your volunteer time must be one week or longer but can extend to more than a month if desired. RV campsites, backcountry camping, and/or dormitory housing may be available.

Sleeping Bear Dunes National Lakeshore

Agency: National Park Service
Season: Summer
Contact: Neil Bullington
9922 Front St.
Empire, MI 49630
Phone: (231) 326–5134

Description/Positions Available: This 71,000-acre park features beech/maple and pine/oak forests, rivers, inland lakes, miles of Lake Michigan beach, two offshore islands, historic farming districts, a lighthouse, one rustic and one modern campground, and 55 miles of hiking trails.

We are looking for people to fill the following positions: Campground Hosts, Photographer, and Maritime Museum and Visitor Center Volunteers. These are needed between spring and fall. We are especially in need of people with natural history backgrounds who can stay all of July and August. An experienced photographer would be employed to document visitor activities and park resources, while we also intend to recruit someone skilled at signing for the hearing impaired. Free campsites may be available. Uniforms are provided. Apply by mid-winter for following season.

Minnesota

Deep-Portage Conservation Reserve

Agency: NON PRO
Season: Summer
Contact: Dale Erger
2197 Nature Center Dr. N.W.
Hackensack, MN 56452
E-mail: portage@uslink.net
Web: www.uslink.net/~portage/
Phone: (218) 682–2325

Description/Positions Available: This 6,000-acre glacial moraine is in northern Minnesota's lakes and forest area, a prime recreation part of the state. The area features 37 miles of trails and a campus with an interpretive center and a conference center.

An Interpretive Naturalist is needed to prepare and present interpretive and environmental education programs for school groups and the general public; host visitors in the interpretive center; and assist professional staff in curriculum development and assessment. Applicants should have background in natural science and possess skills in environmental outdoor education and good public relations. The period of employment is ten weeks. Meals, lodging and a stipend are provided for U.S. residents or travelers with a social security number.

Kekekabic Trail Club

Agency: NON PRO
Season: Spring, Summer, Fall
Contact: Derek Passe
309 Cedar Ave S.
Minneapolis, MN 55454
E-mail: dpasse@spacestar.net
Web: www.keg.org
Phone: (800) 818–4453

Description/Positions Available: The Minnesota Wilderness Trails Alliance offers trail-clearing trips in the Boundary Waters Canoe Area Wilderness. The trips are operated cooperatively by five primary sponsors including the Kekekabic Trail Club.

Using hand tools and teamwork, participants on these trips clear fallen trees and brush from primitive hiking trails in groups of up to nine people. Trips range from weekends to five days, and employ a variety of approaches from backpacking to canoeing, even lodge-based if appropriate. Trail work and travel/camping are conducted under the direction of experienced crew leaders.

Mississippi National River and Recreation Area

Agency: National Park Service
Season: Spring-summer-fall
Contact: Thomas Ibsen
111 E. Kellogg Blvd.
Saint Paul, MN 55101-1256
E-mail: thomas_ibsen@nps.gov
Web: www.nps.gov/miss
Phone: (651) 290–4160

Description/Positions Available: This opportunity is located along the Mississippi River as it passes through the Twin Cities metropolitan area. We need Restoration and Clean-up Specialists for various duties. These include volunteer crews to plant native trees, shrubs, and prairie plants to restore natural vegetation to the river corridor. Volunteers may also remove invasive exotic plants from strategic areas or assist in river corridor cleanups.

Contact us to set up a workday for your group or organization or to learn about existing workdays near you.

Mississippi National River and Recreation Area

Agency: National Park Service
Season: Spring-summer-fall
Contact: Thomas Ibsen
111 E. Kellogg Blvd.
Saint Paul, MN 55101-1256
E-mail: thomas_ibsen@nps.gov
Web: www.nps.gov/miss
Phone: (651) 290–4160

Description/Positions Available: We are recruiting Birding Boat Interpretive Assistants. Volunteers will help Park Rangers to teach bird watching skills to visitors of all ages and, in the process, educate them about the Mississippi River while traveling on a Mississippi River paddleboat. Trips depart from Harriet Island, Saint Paul, and Boom Island during selected weeks within the month of May.

Volunteers will assist at learning stations including "Beaks and adaptations"; "What's Your Wingspan?"; and "Draw Like Audubon." Eight to ten volunteers are needed for each trip.

Mississippi National River and Recreation Area

Agency: National Park Service
Season: Spring-summer-fall
Contact: Thomas Ibsen
111 E. Kellogg Blvd.
Saint Paul, MN 55101-1256
E-mail: thomas_ibsen@nps.gov
Web: www.nps.gov/miss
Phone: (651) 290–4160

Description/Positions Available: Operating on the Mississippi River at Saint Paul, Minnesota, we are recruiting Big River Journey Learning Station Assistants and Monitors. Volunteers will assist Park Rangers with educational learning stations for students in grades four to six onboard a Mississippi River paddleboat. Trips depart daily from Harriet Island, Saint Paul, during selected weeks within the month of May.

Volunteers will assist at learning stations including river geology and ecology. Eight to ten volunteers are needed for each trip.

Mississippi

Bienville National Forest, Bienville District

Agency: U.S. Department of Agriculture Forest Service
Season: Summer
Contact: Eldon Guymon
3473 Hwy. 35 S.
Forest, MS 39074
E-mail: eguymon@fs.fed.us
Web: www.fs.fed.us/r8/miss/
Phone: (601) 469–3811

Description/Positions Available: Located in the east central part of the state, the Bienville National Forest was established in 1934. It was named after the French-Canadian colonist and soldier, Jean Baptiste Bienville, who founded Mobile in 1702, Natchez in 1716, and New Orleans in 1718. Most land acquisitions that later became the Bienville National Forest were directly purchased from four large lumber companies: Adams-Edgar Lumber Company, Bienville Lumber Company, Eastman Gardner Lumber Company, and Marathon Lumber Company.

We intend to locate a volunteer or a couple with an RV or trailer to serve as host(s) for the Shongelo Picnic Area in the summer of 2002. Shongelo contains a five-acre lake with fishing, a pavilion, swimming, and a trail around the edge. Vegetation in the area consists of Southern hardwoods and pine. Spring and fall are lovely in

Mississippi. Summers are warm and humid. Most people in Mississippi still demonstrate Southern hospitality and are very friendly. Full services are available in Brandon located about forty-five minutes north-west of Raleigh. Shongelo is located just north of Raleigh, on State Highway 35.

Desoto National Forest, Chickasawhay District

Agency: U.S. Department of Agriculture Forest Service
Season: Spring, Summer, Fall
Contact: Kim Smith
968 Hwy. 15 S.
Laurel, MS 39443
Phone: (601) 428–0594

Description/Positions Available: This district is located in southern Mississippi close to the beautiful Gulf Coast and offers many cultural, historical and natural resource opportunities.

We are seeking enthusiastic, dependable, and motivated individuals to help provide information to visitors and assist in light maintenance. Facilities are located on the Turkey Fork Reservoir, a beautiful 240-acre lake with good fishing and boating. A

free site with hookups is provided. Hosts are needed between March and November.

Vicksburg National Military Park

Agency: National Park Service
Season: Year-round
Contact: Visitor Protection Supervisor
3201 Clay St.
Vicksburg, MS 39180
E-mail: vick_interpretation@nps.gov
Phone: (601) 636–0583, extension 8055

Description/Positions Available: This park preserves approximately 1,750 acres where General Grant's forces captured Vicksburg in 1863 after a forty-seven-day siege. Sixteen miles of tour road wind through monuments and memorials that mark the Confederate and Union positions.

Volunteers are needed in recreation and resource management. Immediate openings are available for Trail Workers, Fire Technicians, Botanists, Cultural Resource Specialists and Interpretive Specialists.

Missouri

George Washington Carver National Monument

Agency: National Park Service
Season: Year-round
Contact: Ellen M. Cox
5646 Carver Rd.
Diamond, MO 64840
E-mail: ellen_cox@nps.gov
Web: nps.gov/gwca

Description/Positions Available: The park consists of 210 acres of woodlands and prairie with historical structures significant to the boyhood of George Washington Carver. The park

is located 2 miles west of Diamond, Missouri.

Volunteers with experience in horticulture, resource management, maintenance, woodwork, sewing, library science, and computers are especially needed.

Mark Twain National Forest

Agency: U.S. Department of Agriculture Forest Service
Season: Year-round
Contact: Jane Mobley
1104 Walnut St.
Doniphan, MO 63935
E-mail: jmobley@fs.fed.us

Web: www.fs.fed.us/r9marktwain
Phone: (573) 996–2153

Description/Positions Available: Positions are available throughout the Mark Twain National Forest at the following local districts: Ava/Cassville/Willow Springs, Houston/Rolla/Cedar Creek, Salem, Potosi/Fredricktown, Poplar Bluff, and Doniphan/Eleven Point.

Volunteers are required to maintain and host campgrounds, take photographs, plant trees, and seed damaged areas. You will also be able to present environmental education programs, build and repair fences, nesting boxes, picnic tables, and other structures. Building barrier-free campsites, docks, and trails, restoring damaged stream banks and burnt-over areas, and maintaining and inventorying trails are also important roles for which we need volunteer support.

Mark Twain National Forest, Poplar Bluff District

Agency: U.S. Department of Agriculture Forest Service
Season: Summer
Contact: Carolyn Blatz
P.O. Box 988
Poplar Bluff, MO 63901
E-mail: mailroom/r9_marktwain_pb@fs.fed.us
Phone: (573) 785–1475

Description/Positions Available: A Campground Host is needed for Pinewoods Lake Recreation Area. Associated duties include greeting visitors, sharing information, light maintenance, cleanup, and trail work. Law enforcement is provided by the Forest Service and county sheriff's office. We are looking for applicants committed to a minimum stay of thirty days. Some reimbursement of expenses is provided, as is a camping site with electricity, water, hookups and sewer.

Mark Twain National Forest, Potosi, Fredricktown District

Agency: U.S. Department of Agriculture Forest Service
Season: Year-round
Contact: Paul Nazarenko
Hwy. 8 W., Box 188
Potosi, MO 63664
Web: www.fs.fed.us/r9/marktwain/
Phone: (573) 438–5427

Description/Positions Available: This area is famous for its diverse landscapes and is located in the scenic Ozark Mountains. It features connecting ridges, granite knobs, rolling hills, open glades, deep hollows, and cool streams.

Enthusiastic, dependable, and motivated volunteers are sought year-round to serve as Campground Hosts and Groundskeepers, and to perform Ozark Trail Construction, Recreation Area Maintenance, Trail Maintenance, Interpretation, Wilderness Work, Archaeology, Forestry, Visitor Contact, and Carpentry.

Missouri Dept. of Conservation Rockwoods Reservation

Agency: State parks
Season: Year-round
Contact: Tom Meister
2751 Glencoe Rd.
Glencoe, MO 63038
E-mail: meistt@mail.conservation.state.mo.us
Web: www.conservation.state.mo.us
Phone: (636) 458–2236

Description/Positions Available: This 1,898-acre state forest and wildlife refuge, operated by the Missouri Department of Conservation, is located in west St. Louis County and features a conservation education center, hiking trails, and picnic areas. Many educational programs are presented on conservation and the outdoors.

A Volunteer Naturalist is needed to assist with existing programs.

National Park Service/Amtrak

Agency: National Park Service
Season: Year-round
Contact: Mike Corns
11 N. 4th St.
St. Louis, MO 63102
E-mail: Mike_Corns@nps.gov
Phone: (314) 249–7245

Description/Positions Available: See description under Nationwide listings in the front of this directory.

This program is presented on board Amtrak's "Kansas City Mule" between St. Louis and Kansas City, Missouri. We are recruiting Trails & Rails volunteers to ride once a month between these cities. There are no housing, camping, or lodging facilities provided by the program. The only expenses covered are those associated with the actual program.

Ozark National Scenic Riverways

Agency: National Park Service
Season: Summer
Contact: Volunteer Coordinator
P.O. Box 490
Van Buren, MO 63965

E-mail: OZAR_Interpretation@nps.gov
Web: www.nps.gov/ozar
Phone: (573) 323–4236, extension 0

Description/Positions Available: Ozark National Scenic Riverways preserves 184 miles of beautiful free-flowing rivers in south central Missouri. The area is home to the Current and Jacks Fork Rivers, as well as sheer limestone bluffs, rolling hills, springs, and caves. It is heavily rural, with small (under 600 folks) towns and few services. Summers can be hot and humid–all the better reason to get into the water! Campgrounds are intended for families, and the staff makes an effort to include hosts in all social activities. Hosts are provided with a family site and full hookups including water, sewer, and electricity. Prospective applicants are expected to commit at least thirty-two hours per week and work all weekend evenings, as that's when we're busy! Hosts are needed during the period between May 15 and Labor Day weekend each year. Training is provided.

We are recruiting Campground Hosts for Alley Spring, Big Spring, Round Spring, and Pulltite Campgrounds. Hosts are responsible for welcoming campers, performing fee collection activities, and providing a point of contact for campers in the event of emergencies. The job requires a positive attitude, a smile and common sense. Please visit the park Web site to learn more. (www.nps.gov/ozar). For even more information, please click on the "Volunteers" link.

Montana

Bob Marshall Foundation

Agency: NON PRO
Season: Summer
Contact: Carla Cline
P.O. Box 1052
Kalispell, MT 59903
E-mail: carla@bobmarshall.org

Web: www.bobmarshall.org
Phone: (406) 758–5237

Description/Positions Available: The Bob Marshall Foundation is a nonprofit organization that has successfully coordinated projects for the past five years, utilizing hundreds of volunteers to restore trails and preserve wilderness values in the Bob Marshall Wilderness Complex. In that time, more than 1,500 volunteers have worked to clear trails, pull noxious weeds, restore heavily impacted campsites, and participate on trail reconstruction projects.

The Bob Marshall Foundation is currently planning two projects with the American Hiking Society for the summer of 2002. Our Volunteer Vacations project this year takes us to a secondary hiking trail above the South Fork of the Sun River in the Bob Marshall Wilderness. The work on the Prairie–Goat Creek loop will involve clearing windfall, maintaining water bars, brushing, rocking, and minor tread work. Volunteers can also come out and celebrate National Trails Day in early June with the Bob Marshall Foundation. Activities on National Trails Day will include clearing trails with a barbecue at the end of the day. There are many more opportunities to volunteer with the Bob Marshall Foundation throughout the year.

Bureau of Land Management, Miles City Field Office

Agency: Bureau of Land Management
Season: Year-round
Contact: Dan Bricco
111 Garryowen Rd.
Miles City, MT 59301
E-mail: dbricco@mt.blm.gov
Web: www.blm.gov/nhp/index.htm

Description/Positions Available: Located 8 miles east of Miles City, just south of the Yellowstone River, Matthews Recreation Area is a day-use site with an accessible trail, picnic area, and fishing access. The site is along the Lewis and Clark Historic Trail in an area rich in cavalry and Native American history.

Volunteer duties include cleaning one restroom, site clean-up and mowing. Applicants are expected to make a minimum commitment of thirty days stay between April 1 and October 31. The host campsite has power and a septic hookup. A small stipend is also available. We can only employ one individual or couple at a time.

Deerlodge National Forest, Phillipsburg District

Agency: U.S. Department of Agriculture Forest Service
Season: Summer
Contact: Bill Sprauer
88-10A Business Loop
Phillipsburg, MT 59858
Phone: (406) 859–3211

Description/Positions Available: This district features the Anaconda Pintler Wilderness in southwestern Montana and offers outstanding scenery and a wide variety of wildlife.

We are offering positions for two Wilderness Guards (preferably a couple) to work together as a team and perform public contact; provide general information; explain minimum-impact use; and collect information on wilderness conditions for use in updating the management plan. Applicants must be willing and able to backpack into remote areas. Space in a bunkhouse may be available (first come, first served). A small food allowance is provided.

Ennis National Fish Hatchery

Agency: U.S. Department of Agriculture Forest Service
Season: Year-round
Contact: Tom Pruitt
180 Fish Hatchery Rd.
Ennis, MT 59729
E-mail: tom_a_pruitt@fws.gov
Web: www.r6.fws.gov/hatchery/ennis/ennis.html
Phone: (406) 682–4847

Description/Positions Available: Ennis National Fish Hatchery is the largest trout broodstock facility in the federal hatchery system. Located in the scenic Madison Valley, northwest of Yellowstone Park and near the world-famous Madison River, the area provides unlimited trout fishing and many other outdoor opportunities.

Fishery Technicians are needed to assist the hatchery staff in sorting and spawning six strains of rainbow trout, shocking, treating, picking, and shipping eggs, plus other hatchery activities as called for. A bunkhouse is available, alongside a daily food stipend of $15. The tour of duty is a forty-hour, five-day week. Some weekends or holidays may be worked with days off during the week. Volunteers are needed throughout the year, with peak periods from October to March. We prefer a minimum of six weeks employment.

Flathead National Forest, Spotted Bear District

Agency: U.S. Department of Agriculture Forest Service
Season: Summer
Contact: Alan Koss
Box 190310
Hungry Horse, MT 59919
E-mail: Akoss@fs.fed.us
Phone: (406) 387–3860

Description/Positions Available: Wilderness Ranger Assistants are needed in the Bob Marshall Wilderness. Duties include providing visitor contact; assisting in wilderness-monitoring projects; rehabilitating wilderness campsites; and maintaining trails and facilities. Volunteers will be required to be on the trail for predetermined patrols. Due to the remoteness of duty stations, which require one or two days of travel each way, volunteers usually spend days off in the wilderness and return to district headquarters only once or twice during the season. Grizzly bear awareness, stock-handling and first-aid training are provided. This position requires the ability to write simple reports and communicate effectively with wilderness visitors, plus the physical conditioning to carry at least a fifty-lb. backpack in a rugged wilderness setting. Preference will be afforded to those with knowledge of stock-handling techniques, recreation management, environmental education, biology, natural science, or geology.

Personal transportation is desirable.

Kootenai National Forest, Fortine District

Agency: U.S. Department of Agriculture Forest Service
Contact: David B. Nesbitt
Box 116
Fortine, MT 59918
E-mail: dbnesbitt@fs.fed.us
Web: www.gorp.com/gorp/resource/US_ National_ Forest/mt/mt_koote_4.htm
Phone: (406) 882–4451

Description/Positions Available: This district features the proposed Ten Lakes Wilderness and Thompson-Seton Roadless Area and is home to numerous high mountain lakes, wildflowers, huckleberries, and a variety of wildlife species.

Trail Crew Members are needed to work with an experienced trail crew and with youth conservation crew members to clear trails using primitive tools. Duties include building footbridges, placing directional signs, and assisting in campground maintenance work. You must be in excellent physical condition, willing to work in adverse conditions, and enjoy working with people. Volunteers need high-top leather boots and some camping gear.

Lolo National Forest

Agency: U.S. Department of Agriculture Forest Service
Season: Summer
Contact: Joe Kipphut
Bldg. 24-A, Fort Missoula
Missoula, MT 59804
E-mail: jkipphut@fs.fed.us
Web: www.fs.fed.us/r1/lolo

Description/Positions Available: Pattee Canyon Campground is located 3.5 miles southeast of Missoula on a paved county road.

Campground Hosts are needed from Memorial

Day to Labor Day. Telephone, septic, and electricity hookups are all provided. Propane is also paid for, while water is trucked in. There are twenty-two family sites and three group sites at an elevation of 4,200 feet. Money handling is not part of the host's duties. The host site and surrounding roads are shaded and double wide paved.

Lolo National Forest, Ninemile District

Agency: U.S. Department of Agriculture Forest Service
Season: Summer
Contact: Volunteer Coordinator
20325 Remount Rd.
Huson, MT 59846
Phone: (406) 626–5201

Description/Positions Available: The historic Ninemile Remount Depot is located about 25 miles west of Missoula near Huson. This secluded but beautiful mountainous area is full of wildlife and recreation opportunities.

We are seeking Visitor Center Information Hosts. Applicants' responsibilities will include greeting visitors, providing information about local attractions and history, and occasionally leading guided tours around the depot. During slow periods, volunteers may be asked to help with district projects such as stuffing envelopes and copying. A camper trailer site complete with full hookups is provided. The visitor center is open from Memorial Day to Labor Day. Actual workdays can be flexible to meet volunteers' needs. A friendly manner and good communication skills are essential. On-the-job orientation and training are provided. We also need Campground Hosts. Trailer pads are provided for volunteers for this position but no hookups.

Missoula Field Office, Bureau of Land Management

Agency: Bureau of Land Management
Season: Summer
Contact: Dick Fichtler
Bureau of Land Management 3255

Fort Missoula Rd.
Missoula, MT 59804
E-mail: Richard_Fichtler@blm.gov
Web: www.mt.blm.gov/mifo/

Volunteers are needed at Garnet Ghost Town to assist with interpreting the history of Garnet Ghost Town. Volunteers would also have the opportunity to participate in maintaining Garnet's historic structures and to work on the many trails in this area.

Opportunities are available for Visitor Center Hosts, Historic Building Maintenance Workers in a ghost town, and those interested in general trail maintenance.

Montana/Dakotas State Office

Agency: Bureau of Land Management
Season: Summer
Contact: Volunteer Program Coordinator
Box 36800, 5001 Southgate Dr.
Billings, MT 59107
Web: www.mt.blm.gov/
Phone: (406) 896–5230

Description/Positions Available: Campground Hosts are needed for several field office locations in both Montana and North and South Dakota. The sites vary and specific locations can be obtained by calling the Volunteer Coordinator. Hookups for personal camping trailers are available; however travel expenses to and from Montana and North and South Dakota are not included.

National Park Service/Amtrak

Agency: National Park Service
Season: Summer
Contact: Laurie Heupel
P.O. Box 1806
Great Falls, MT 59403
E-mail: Laurie_Heupel@nps.gov
Phone: (406) 727–8733, extension 311

Description/Positions Available: See description under Nationwide listings in the front of this directory.

This program is presented on board Amtrak's "Empire Builder" between Seattle, Washington, and Havre, Montana. Trails & Rails volunteers are required to ride once a month between these cities. There are no housing, camping, or lodging facilities provided by the program. The only expenses covered are those associated with the actual program.

The Nature Center at Fort Missoula

Agency: The Nature Center at Fort Missoula
Season: Year-round
Contact: Katie MacMillen
Post Headquarters, Bldg. T-2,
Fort Missoula Rd.
Missoula, MT 59804
E-mail: mnhc@montana.com
Web: www.TheNatureCenter.org
Phone: (406) 327–0405

Description/Positions Available: The Nature Center at Fort Missoula is an environmental education organization, teaching day care to seniors and fostering understanding, appreciation, and conservation of natural systems through natural history education in the northern Rocky Mountains region.

Volunteer opportunities include: helping docents teach natural history, maintaining the native plant Nature Adventure Playground by planting, weeding and designing further additions, leading children in summer nature day care and summer science days, organizing and supporting our spring watershed festival and fall fundraising auction, accompanying expert volunteers, staff, visitors on nature walks and Elderhostel presentations, checking and updating our traveling educational trunks, updating library checkouts and returns, creating passive and interactive museum exhibits, cleaning and occasionally painting the building, and helping with day-to-day administration and errands.

Nebraska

Nebraska National Forest

Agency: U.S. Department of Agriculture Forest Service
Season: May 27 to October 16
Contact: Patti Barney
P.O. Box 38
Halsey, NE 69142
Phone: (308) 533–2257

Description/Positions Available: In the heart of the beautiful and rural Nebraska sandhills, this man-made forest is often described as an oasis of trees in a sea of grass. A small town with groceries, tavern, and gas is nearby.

Campground Hosts are needed from May 27 to October 16 or later for a developed recreation area that includes a campground, picnic area, swimming pool, arboretum, tennis courts and horseshoe-pitching area. Duties include providing information to forest visitors, keeping records of campground use, and performing clean-up and maintenance duties. Applicants must enjoy talking to and helping people and be in good physical condition. You also require your own camper/RV and personal transportation. Benefits include a campsite with full hookups, a storage shed, showers, laundry facilities, a garden spot, and $6.00 per diem subsistence. A Tour Guide is also needed from April 18 to May 27 to lead tours composed of people of all ages around the oldest federal nursery in the United States and an operating fire look-out tower. From this site visitors can view the largest hand-planted forest in the Western Hemisphere. Some light maintenance work may also be involved. You must enjoy talking to people, especially children, and be in good physical condition. You also require your own camper/RV and vehicle. Benefits include $6.00 per day subsistence, hookups, showers, and laundry facilities.

Nevada

Bureau of Land Management, Elko Field Office

Agency: Bureau of Land Management
Season: Summer
Contact: Steve Dondero
3900 E. Idaho St.
Elko, NV 89801
Web: www.nv.blm.gov
Phone: (775) 653–0200

Description/Positions Available: Wilson Reservoir Campground is located in northeastern Nevada, approximately 90 miles northwest of Elko. This is a Bureau of Land Management campground in a remote location in the sagebrush country of the Great Basin Desert. The campground consists of twenty campsites with tables and fire rings, a day-use area, boat ramp, hand pump water, vault toilets, and dirt roads. Including the reservoir, this management area covers 5,440 acres. Fees are charged for camping and use of the boat ramp. The reservoir sits at approximately 5,300 feet in elevation with temperatures ranging from daytime highs of seventy-five to ninety-five degrees Fahrenheit and nighttime lows to forty degrees Fahrenheit (May through September).

North Wildhorse Campground is located in northeastern Nevada, approximately 70 miles north of Elko. This is a Bureau of Land Management campground located off Highway 225 just north of Wild Horse Reservoir in the sagebrush country of the Great Basin Desert. The campground consists of eighteen campsites with tables; fire rings; shade ramadas and/or aspen trees; three group sites; hand pump water; vault toilets; and gravel roads. Campground is open late May through October. Fees are charged for camping. The campground sits at approximately 6,200 feet in elevation with temperatures ranging from day time highs of seventy to ninety degrees

Fahrenheit and nighttime lows to thirty five degrees Fahrenheit (May through September).

Campground Hosts are needed at both sites from Memorial Day to Labor Day weekend. Duties include public contact, fee collection, cleaning restrooms, litter pickup, and first aid (training provided). Compensation includes per diem and free camping.

Bureau of Land Management, Ely Field Office

Agency: Bureau of Land Management
Season: Year-round
Contact: Gretchen Burris
HC 33 Box 33500
Ely, NV 89301
E-mail: gretchen_burris@nv.blm.gov
Web: www.nv.blm.gov/Ely
Phone: (775) 289–1800

Description/Positions Available: The Ely District is located within both the Great Basin and the Mojave Desert areas of Nevada. The District includes 12 million acres, with 1.25 million acres distributed among twenty-five Wilderness Study Areas and Instant Study Areas. These areas range in size from 3,000 acres to 180,000 acres and cover a variety of terrain and vegetation types. The vegetation types range from joshua tree/blackbrush/creosote to sagebrush/grasslands to pinyon/juniper to high elevation stands of aspen, mahogany, white fire and bristlecone pine. The elevations range from 3,000 to nearly 11,000 feet. The town of Ely is a full-service community of 5,000 located 250 miles north of Las Vegas and 250 miles southwest of Salt Lake City.

The Ely District needs volunteers to perform wilderness monitoring. Duties include: Reviewing and updating wilderness files and reports, monitoring individual wilderness and Instant Study areas through driving and hiking the boundaries and hiking the interiors, marking WSA boundaries, taking photos, and documenting any unauthorized activities. Volunteers must be prepared to work in remote areas with limited communications. Volunteers will camp out four to five days per week and will often work alone. Volunteers who can only work limited periods of time, such as weekends, are welcome. Mapping skills/GPS/GIS are highly desired. Training available. Camping gear/4WD vehicle can be provided. No housing is available during the winter. Primitive housing may be available from spring to fall.

Bureau of Land Management, State Office

Agency: Bureau of Land Management
Season: Year-round
Contact: Debra Kolkman
1340 Financial Blvd.
Reno, NV 89502
Web: www.nv.blm.gov/
Phone: (775) 289–1946

Description/Positions Available: Within the State of Nevada, almost forty-eight million acres of public land are administered by the Bureau of Land Management, an agency of the U.S. Department of the Interior. The lands cover 67 percent of the area of the state.

We are looking for volunteers statewide. Please call or visit our Web site for volunteer opportunities and locations.

Cathedral Gorge State Park

Agency: State parks
Season: Year-round
Contact: Park Supervisor
P.O. Box 176
Panaca, NV 89042
E-mail: cathedralgorge_vc@leturbonet.com
Web: www.state.nv.us/stparks/
Phone: (775) 728–4460

Description/Positions Available: This scenic

small park has geologic formations that remind many visitors of the hoodoos and spires of the Badlands or Bryce National Park. Hiking trails lead through a maze of slot canyons and open, high desert terrain.

Positions are available for Campground Hosts; Visitor Center or Interpretive Assistants; and those interested in trail maintenance. We are sorry, but Nevada State Parks do not offer a stipend to volunteers; a free campsite will be provided during the volunteer's length of stay (no hookups available).

Desert National Wildlife Refuge Complex

Agency: U.S. Fish and Wildlife Service
Season: Year-round
Contact: Callie Leau Courtwright
1500 North Decatur Blvd.
Las Vegas, NV 89178
Phone: (702) 646–3401

Description/Positions Available: This isolated refuge is located approximately 100 miles North of Las Vegas near the small rural community of Alamo (population 400, elevation 3,500 feet, temperature 10 to 100 degrees Fahrenheit). Services are limited but recreational opportunities abound. The habitat on the 5,380-acre refuge is primarily wetland and riparian areas surrounded by rugged Mojave/Great Basin Desert scrub. The refuge provides important nesting habitat for resident and migratory waterfowl, shorebirds and passerines and is an important staging area for other migrants.

Conservation Volunteer(s) positions are available. Duties include assisting in biological investigations, revegetation projects, cultural/historical investigations, visitor services, and maintenance/construction activities. Duties will be tailored to the experience and interest of individual volunteers. Bunkhouse facilities are available. Trailer pads are also available at no cost to volunteers. A $10 per diem stipend is paid to all volunteers. Call or write for a volunteer application form.

Humboldt-Toiyabe National Forest

Agency: U.S. Department of Agriculture Forest Service
Season: Summer
Contact: David Ashby, Recreation Forester
P.O. Box 246, 140 Pacific Ave.
Wells, NV 89835
E-mail: dashby@fs.fed.us
Web: www.fs.fed.us/htnf/
Phone: (775) 752-3357

Description/Positions Available: Northeast Nevada Group: Ruby Mountains Ranger District (Wells, Nevada); Jarbidge Ranger District (Wells, Nevada); Mountain City Ranger District (Elko, Nevada); Santa Rosa Ranger District (Winnemucca, Nevada)
Wilderness Ranger Assistants (two); Trail Maintenance Crew members (four)

Humboldt-Toiyabe National Forest, Ely Ranger District

Agency: U.S. Department of Agriculture Forest Service
Season: Summer
Contact: Barbara C. Walker
350 8th St.
Ely, NV 89301
E-mail: bcwalker@fs.fed.us
Phone: (775) 289-3031

Description/Positions Available: We have three remote guard stations that we are interested in having occupied for the summer season. We would be interested in having some maintenance work done by a volunteer, such as scraping or painting of facilities, or watering horse pastures. Volunteers are also needed to occupy three remote guard stations.

Tahoe Rim Trail Association

Agency: NON PRO
Season: Summer
Contact: Sara Holm
P.O. Box 4647
Stateline, NV 89449
E-mail: tahoerimtrail@aol.com
Web: www.tahoerimtrail.org
Phone: (775) 588-0686

Description/Positions Available: The 150-mile Tahoe Rim Trail circles Lake Tahoe along the ridges and mountaintops that form the Lake Tahoe basin. This trail winds through two states (California and Nevada), six counties, three national forests, state parkland, and three wilderness areas.
Trail Builders and Trail Maintainers are needed to help with re-routes and other exciting preservation projects on this beautiful trail.

New Hampshire

Lake Umbagog National Wildlife Refuge

Agency: U.S. Fish and Wildlife Service
Season: Summer
Contact: Laurie Wunder
P.O. Box 240
Errol, NH 03579
E-mail: FW5RW_LUNWR@fws.gov
Phone: (603) 482-3415

Description/Positions Available: Lake Umbagog NWR is located in a remote setting 6 miles north of Errol, New Hampshire, without public transportation to services. A personal vehicle is therefore essential. We expect volunteers to work forty hours per week including some weekends and holidays. We will provide a $200 weekly stipend and housing.

We offer one position for wildlife monitors (frogs, birds, bats, small mammals). This begins approximately May 6, 2002. One vegetation survey position is also available, alongside one environmental/public use position beginning approximately June 3, 2002. All positions run until August 23, 2002. Please request a more comprehensive list of opportunities and application instructions. Evaluations begin approximately February 1, 2002. Positions will remain open until filled.

Saco Ranger District, White Mountain National Forest

Agency: U.S. Department of Agriculture Forest Service
Season: Summer
Contact: Susan Spruce
33 Kancamagus Hwy.
Conway, NH 03818
E-mail: sspruceeland@fs.fed.us
Web: www.fs.fed.us/r9/white/
Phone: (603) 447–5448

Description/Positions Available: You will be based in the Saco District of the White Mountain National Forest, Conway, New Hampshire. The Russell-Colbath Historic Homestead is located 12 miles west on the Kancamagus Highway from Conway. The Kancamagus is one of the twelve most scenic byways in the United States. The house is a small cape, which is listed on the National Register of Historic Places. It was built in 1832 and includes a petite herb and vegetable garden with a 0.7 mile nature trail behind the house. We handle around 10,000 visitors in five months.

We are looking for a good-natured individual or couple to work three days a week at the historic homestead from Memorial Day weekend to Columbus Day. This position compensates the

volunteer(s) with $25 per diem. Volunteers interpret the history of the area, the people who once resided in it, and the unique events that occurred there during the early part of the twentieth century. Managing daily donations, daily light housekeeping, raking, gardening, and toilet cleaning are required. Baking, making stews, and interpretive programs are welcome.

White Mountain National Forest

Agency: U.S. Department of Agriculture Forest Service
Season: Year-round
Contact: Sterling Messer
P.O. Box 15, Rte. 175
Plymouth , NH 03264
E-mail: smesser@fs.fed.us
Web: www.fs.fed.us/r9/white/
Phone: (603) 536–1315

Description/Positions Available: The positions are in the White Mountain National Forest in central/northern New Hampshire and western Maine.

We need Visitor Information Services folks, Light and Heavy Maintenance volunteers and Trail Maintenance assistants. We are also looking for people to maintain signs, patrol parking lots for care and police, maintain restrooms, help administer day use areas, engage in light and medium construction work, vehicle and equipment maintenance, painting, interpretive program presenting, office work, cross-country ski trail packing, winter trails maintenance work, and photography. If you have a skill or see a need for a job to be done in your national forest, we are willing to talk to you. There are a limited number of full-amenity campsites available for summer season volunteers and limited housing opportunities for year-round workers.

New Jersey

Great Swamp National Wildlife Refuge

Agency: U.S. Fish and Wildlife Service
Season: Year-round
Contact: Tom Mcfadden
152 Pleasant Plains Rd.
Basking Ridge, NJ 07920
E-mail: tom_mcfadden@fws.gov
Phone: (973) 425–1222, extension 14

Description/Positions Available: Great Swamp is a 7,500-acre National Wildlife Refuge located in Morris County, New Jersey.

Interns assist in all aspects of refuge management including maintenance, biological programs and surveys, deer hunt, visitor assistance, trail work and office work. Position includes housing and a stipend of $140 weekly. Applicants should submit a resume and state what season they are looking for. Starting dates are June, September, and January. Positions last twelve weeks.

Palisades Interstate Park

Agency: State parks
Season: Year-round
Contact: Eric Nelsen
P.O. Box 155
Alpine, NJ 07620
E-mail: bkhouse@njpalisades.org
Web: www.njpalisades.org

The 2,500-acre New Jersey Section of the Palisades Interstate Park lies on the west shore of the Hudson River between the George Washington Bridge and the New York state line. Noted for its sheer cliffs and scenic views, the park contains picnic areas, boat basins, historic sites, a nature sanctuary, 30 miles of hiking and cross-country ski trails and scenic roads.

We have year-round and seasonal opportunities in cultural, historical, environmental, educational, recreational, informational and operational services. Routine positions ranging from general maintenance to visitor services are also available. No housing can be provided at this time.

Wallkill River National Wildlife Refuge

Agency: U.S. Fish and Wildlife Service
Season: Spring to fall
Contact: Refuge Operations Specialist
1547 County Rte. 565
Susses, NJ 07471
Phone: (973) 702–7266

Description/Positions Available: Located in the northwestern corner of the state, this refuge encompasses a variety of habitats, including riverine wetlands, emergent marshes, flooded wetlands, grasslands, and hardwood forests. The Appalachian Trail traverses the northern section of the refuge.

A Volunteer Botanist is needed to monitor vegetation and identify wildflowers. Dormitory-style housing with kitchens and bath facilities is available. Volunteer Trail Workers are required to maintain dirt trails, build boardwalk, and construct wildlife observation platforms. Tours of duty can range from a week to six months.

New Mexico

Aztec Ruins National Monument

Agency: National Park Service
Season: Year-round
Contact: Volunteer Coordinator
84 County Rd. 2900
Aztec, NM 87410
Phone: (505) 334–6174

Description/Positions Available: Located in the heart of the "Four Corners" country, this monument preserves a prehistoric Anasazi pueblo ruin occupied from A.D. 1100 to 1300. The area includes a reconstructed Great Kiva and Chaco/Mesa Verde-style great house, the Ruins Trail (400 yards long), a museum, and a picnic area.

An Interpretation/Visitor Services Volunteer is needed for information desk, trail patrol, and interpretive talks. Experience dealing with the public is preferred. Call or write for training session dates and other details. We also need a Maintenance Worker for groundskeeping and custodial work. Housing is not available.

Bureau of Land Management, Taos

Agency: Bureau of Land Management
Season: Year-round
Contact: Guadalupe Martinez
Bureau of Land Management-Taos 226 Cruz Alta Rd.
Taos, NM 87571
E-mail: guadalupe.martinez@hotmail.com
Web: www.nm.blm.gov/www/tafo_home.html
Phone: (505) 758–8851

Description/Positions Available: The majestic Rio Grande Gorge begins just north of the Colorado border and continues south into New Mexico about 70 miles. Its spectacular views, rich history, and varied opportunities for hiking, whitewater rafting, fishing, bicycling and birding make it a popular year-round destination for visitors and residents alike. Orilla Verde Recreation Area south of Taos is nestled in the Rio Grande Gorge, with facilities along the banks of the Rio Grande. The Wild Rivers Recreation Area north of Taos has facilities located on the rim of the 800-foot deep Gorge, with several miles of trails providing access to the river below. Four other areas provide easy access to the river for boating, fishing, and swimming; one site is a popular hot spring next to the Rio Grande.

We are recruiting Campground Hosts to help with visitor services at the campgrounds and two visitor centers, assist with some maintenance, and collect fees. River Hosts work at key access points to the Rio Grande, providing information, monitoring commercial and private boating uses, performing some maintenance and some traffic control. If you are interested in this position, please get in touch. Limited housing is available, so volunteers are encouraged to provide their own RV. We provide hookups and subsistence pay.

Capulin National Monument

Agency: National Park Service
Season: Year-round
Contact: Ruben Andrade
P.O.Box 40
Capulin, NM 88414
E-mail: ruben_andrade@nps.gov
Phone: (505) 278–2201, ext. 231
Web: www.nps.gov/cavo/index.htm

Description/Positions Available: Capulin Volcano, which erupted approximately 60,000 years ago, is part of the easternmost volcanic field in Northern America. It was proclaimed a National Monument in 1961. The monument preserves the nearly perfect Capulin cinder cone, which rises more than 1,000 feet above the surrounding landscape.

Volunteers are needed to staff the visitor center and greet visitors, collect fees, and provide park orientation. We also need volunteers to work with the Maintenance and Resource Management Divisions on various projects. There are two RV pads with full hookups.

Carlsbad Caverns National Park

Agency: National Park Service
Season: Year-round
Contact: Volunteer Coordinator
3225 National Parks Hwy.
Carlsbad, NM 88220
E-mail: cave_volunteers@nps.gov
Web: www.nps.gov/cave

Description/Positions Available: In addition to Carlsbad Cavern, this park of over 46,000 acres preserves more than ninety-four known caves and a very scenic and rugged portion of Chihuahuan desert.

Special opportunities are available for persons interested in natural resources, including working in deserts and caves and working with the public. Some trail improvement projects are suitable for groups. Dorm-style housing is provided, as well as training and uniforms (as needed).

Carson National Park, Questa Ranger District

Agency: U.S. Department of Agriculture Forest Service
Season: Summer
Contact: Mary Ann Elder
P.O. Box 110
Questa, NM 87556
E-mail: melder@fs.fed.us
Web: www.gorp.com/gorp/resource/US_National_Forest/nm/nm_carso_4.htm
Phone: (505) 586–0520

Description/Positions Available: Goose Lake Trail is in the Columbine/Hondo Wilderness Study Area. The project begins at Goose Lake and ascends 1,000 feet to Gold Hill (about 12,600 feet). All of the trail is above the tree line.

We are looking for a crew of between ten and thirty people. The crew will complete switchbacks through a talus slope and rehabilitate the old trail alignment. Camping is available at Goose Lake, but this is only accessible by high clearance 4x4 vehicles. Gold Hill is a prominent landmark, visible from Wheeler Peak and Taos Ski Valley.

Gila Cliff Dwellings National Monument

Agency: National Park Service
Season: Year-round
Contact: Douglas Ballou
HC 68, Box 100
Silver City, NM 88061
Phone: (505) 536–9461

Description/Positions Available: This monument, located in the heart of the 600,000-acre Gila Wilderness, is operated for the National Park Service by the USDA Forest Service. The facility includes the 700-year-old Mogollon cliff dwellings, four campgrounds, scenic overlooks, access to more than 700 miles of wilderness trails, and a visitor center that serves both wilderness users and cliff dwelling visitors. Recreational opportunities include hiking and backpacking, horse trails, kayaking, wilderness hot springs, wildlife observation, and outstanding solitude.

Campground Hosts are needed year-round to perform light maintenance and cleaning of facilities, camper contacts and assistance, and to organize resource conservation activities. Interpretation volunteers are also needed to conduct research and provide interpretation of the cliff dwellings and surrounding forest ecosystem. Positions are also available for Visitor Center staff. Duties include providing wilderness, cliff dwelling, and area information to visitors. Maintenance volunteer opportunities exist for various field, shop, and carpentry projects. The main visitor season is from May to October, but year-round needs exist. Campground Hosts must supply their own trailer/RV and will utilize a remote fixed dump station. Limited housing may be available including trailer pads with partial hookups and dorm space for other volunteers.

Pecos National Historical Park

Agency: National Park Service
Season: Year-round
Contact: Volunteer Coordinator
P.O. Box 418
Pecos, NM 87552
Phone: (505) 757–6414, extension 1

Description/Positions Available: This park preserves the ruins of the fifteenth-century Pecos Pueblo and the ruins of a seventeenth/eighteenth-century Spanish Franciscan Mission. Just 25 miles from Santa Fe, it is near the entrance to Santa Fe National Forest and Pecos Wilderness, where opportunities for camping, hiking, and fishing abound.

Volunteers are needed for Visitor Orientation, Guided Tours, and Resource Management.

Pecos–Las Vegas Ranger District

Agency: U.S. Department of Agriculture Forest Service
Season: Summer
Contact: Toby Gass
P.O .Drawer 429
Pecos, NM 87552
E-mail: tgass@fs.fed.us
Web: pecosnewmexico.com/index.html
Phone: (505) 757–6121

Description/Positions Available: The Pecos Wilderness is a high-altitude alpine wilderness area in northern New Mexico. It is characterized by lakes, streams, spruce forest, large open meadows, and 12,000-foot peaks. Summers are characterized by warm days and cool nights,

with frequent severe thunderstorms from mid-July to mid-August. In a normal snowfall year, snowmelt occurs in May with the first major snow of the year typically occurring in mid-October. The wilderness is used by both hikers and equestrians. The wilderness is located in northern New Mexico, between Santa Fe and Las Vegas, and is bounded by centuries-old Hispanic villages. The Ranger District offices are located in the village of New Mexico. The nearest larger city is Santa Fe, approximately 25 miles away.

We are recruiting Wilderness Trail Workers. Duties include performing trail maintenance and reconstruction in a high-altitude alpine wilderness using hand tools and traditional skills. This work requires hiking, backpacking, and horsepacking skills.

Pecos–Las Vegas Ranger District

Agency: U.S. Department of Agriculture Forest Service
Season: Summer
Contact: Toby Gass
P.O. Drawer 429
Pecos, NM 87552
E-mail: tgass@fs.fed.us
Web: pecosnewmexico.com/index.html
Phone: (505) 757–6121

Description/Positions Available: The Pecos Wilderness is a high-altitude alpine wilderness area in northern New Mexico, approximately one hour from Santa Fe. The Wilderness is characterized by lakes, streams, spruce forest, large open meadows, and 12,000-foot peaks. Summers are characterized by warm days and cool nights, with frequent severe thunderstorms from mid-July to mid-August. In a normal snowfall year, snowmelt occurs in May with the first major snow of the year typically occurring in mid-October. The Wilderness is used by both hikers and equestrians. The Wilderness is located in northern New Mexico, between

Santa Fe and Las Vegas, and is bounded by centuries-old Hispanic villages. The Ranger District offices are located in the village of New Mexico. The nearest larger city is Santa Fe, approximately 25 miles away.

We require Wilderness Patrol Workers. This involves spending extended periods of time in the Pecos Wilderness, contacting members of the public, cleaning campsites, documenting conditions, recording trail inventory information, collecting GPS data, doing minor trail maintenance, replacing signs, etc. A packhorse is available for longer patrols (for those who attend training or already have the skills). Positions are available in both summer and fall. This work requires excellent physical condition and outdoors skills.

Data collection positions are also available for individuals with the necessary GPS/GIS skills to perform basic data gathering and entry of trails and visitor use information. These are field-going positions, which require the same level of outdoor skills as the above wilderness patrol positions. Individuals should be willing to spend days sitting at fixed points along the trails, recording visitor use data. These positions require dayhiking rather than backpacking.

White Sands National Monument

Agency: National Park Service
Season: Year-round
Contact: John Mangimeli
P.O. Box 1086
Holloman AFB, NM 88330
E-mail: john_mangimeli@nps.gov
Web: www.nps.gov/whsa

Phone: (505) 679–2599

Description/Positions Available: An experienced Web Page Developer is needed to maintain and upgrade the Web page of one of the world's great scenic wonders. RV spaces are available. Housing may be available during certain times of the year. One position is needed, anytime between November and April, with at least a two-month commitment.

White Sands National Monument

Agency: National Park Service
Season: Winter
Contact: John Mangimeli
P.O. Box 1086
Holloman AFB, NM 88330
E-mail: john_mangimeli@nps.gov
Web: www.nps.gov/whsa
Phone: (505) 679–2599

Description/Positions Available: This National Park Service area preserves the world's largest gypsum dune field and unique plants and animals that have adapted to it. It is known for its spectacular scenery, mild winter climate, and numerous opportunities for outdoor recreation in both desert and mountains.

A Volunteer Interpreter is needed. You will educate the public about the geology and ecology of the area, through formal interpretive programs, nature walks, and staffing the information desk. Training, housing, utilities, and a food stipend are all provided.

New York

Finger Lakes National Forest

Agency: U.S. Department of Agriculture Forest Service
Season: Year-round
Contact: Kathleen Diehl
231 North Main St.
Rutland, VT 05701
E-mail: kdiehl@fs.fed.us
Web: www.fs.fed.us/r9/gmfl/
Phone: (802) 747–6709

Description/Positions Available: The forest's scenic beauty along the ridges between Cayuga Lake and Seneca Lake offer unlimited recreation opportunities any season of the year. Whether you are a hiker, skier, camper, fishing or hunting enthusiast, or wildlife watcher, the Finger Lakes National Forest can provide the recreational experience you are seeking!

Frontliners help in visitor information centers to greet people, answer phone calls, and distribute information to potential visitors. We need six Campground Hosts. We also use Environmental Assessment volunteers to work with Forest Planning on the new revision of the Forest Management Plan. Volunteers should have at least basic knowledge of environmental assessments. We also always need Trail Maintenance volunteers.

Finger Lakes National Forest, Hector Ranger District

Agency: U.S. Department of Agriculture Forest Service
Season: Summer
Contact: Chris Zimmer
5218 State Rte. 414
Hector, NY 14841
E-mail: czimmer@fs.fed.us
Web: www.fs.fed.us/r9/gmfl

Phone: (607) 546–4470

Description/Positions Available: A Campground Host is needed in New York's only national forest. Surrounded by two of the most beautiful of New York's Finger Lakes, three campgrounds provide hosting opportunities, one devoted exclusively to horseback riders. The site is close to the NASCAR racing at Watkins Glen International Racetrack, Ithaca, New York, and to the bountiful wineries along the shores of Seneca and Cayuga Lakes.

A stipend of $10 per diem is provided for the host.

Finger Lakes Trail Conference

Agency: NON PRO
Season: Summer
Contact: Howard Beye
202 Colebourne Rd.
Rochester, NY 14609
E-mail: fltc@frontiernet.net
Web: www.fingerlakes.net/trailsystem

Description/Positions Available: We operate along the Finger Lakes Trail and North Country Trail, central New York, near Ellicottville. Base camp will be at the forty-five-acre Finger Lakes Trail Conference property at the project site. Volunteers are needed for a crew to construct a 30-foot beam bridge over Devereaux Creek. Crew members will camp in their own tents. Meals and camping will be provided at no charge to volunteers.

We are looking for a Construction Crew for bridge building. Experience with tools and construction is helpful but not required. You will work between August 12 and 16. There will be around ten crew members.

Finger Lakes Trail Conference

Agency: NON PRO
Season: Summer
Contact: Howard Beye
202 Colebourne Rd.
Rochester, NY 14609
E-mail: fltc@frontiernet.net
www.fingerlakes.net/trailsystem

Description/Positions Available: We are working on the Finger Lakes Trail, central New York, near Genesee River, performing general trail improvements.

We want to recruit a crew of up to ten volunteers, working June 17 to 21. Lodging will be in a cabin at Camp Sam Wood, near Pike, New York, on Wiscoy Creek (well known for its trout fishing). Meals and lodgings are provided at no cost.

Finger Lakes Trail Conference

Agency: NON PRO
Season: Fall
Contact: Howard Beye
202 Colebourne Rd.
Rochester, NY 14609
E-mail: fltc@frontiernet.net
Web: www.fingerlakes.net/trailsystem

Description/Positions Available: Finger Lakes Trail/North Country Trail, western New York, Allegany State Park. A volunteer crew will work September 16 to 20. Lodging will be in park cabins. Meals and lodging will be provided at no cost to volunteers.

Volunteers will form a Trail Crew to do trail improvement work on the parts of the FLT/NCT within the state park. This will involve reducing slope angles and moving the trail away from wet areas. The crew will consist of about ten persons.

Iroquois National Wildlife Refuge

Agency: U.S. Fish and Wildlife Service
Season: Spring
Contact: Dorothy Gerhart
1101 Casey Rd.
Basom, NY 14013
Web: iroquoisnwr.fws.gov/
Phone: (716) 948–5445

Description/Positions Available: The refuge has 10,818 acres of diverse habitat, which is managed for waterfowl and other migratory birds as well as resident wildlife. Nature trails, overlooks, and canoeing in Oak Orchard Creek provide wildlife observation opportunities.

We are recruiting the following: Visitor Center Assistant, Naturalist Interpreter, Facilities Maintenance worker (trails, overlooks, landscaping, mowing).

National Park Service/Amtrak

Agency: National Park Service
Season: Summer
Contact: Trails & Rails Coordinator
648 Rte. 32
Stillwater, NY 12170
E-mail: Interpretation_SARA@nps.gov
Phone: (518) 664–9821

Description/Positions Available: See description under Nationwide listings in the front of this directory.

This program is presented on board Amtrak's "Adirondack" between Albany and Westport, New York. We need Trails & Rails volunteers to ride once a month between these cities. There are no housing, camping, or lodging facilities provided by the program. The only expenses covered are those associated with the actual program.

North Carolina

Blue Ridge Parkway

Agency: National Park Service
Season: Summer
Contact: Volunteer Coordinator
199 Hemphill Knob Rd.
Asheville, NC 28803
E-mail: patty_lockamy@nps.gov
Web: www.nps.gov/blri

Description/Positions Available: The Blue Ridge Parkway is a 469-mile scenic roadway and national park area stretching through the heart of the Appalachian Mountains in North Carolina and Virginia.

The park utilizes volunteers in many aspects of serving the public and preserving the natural and cultural resources of the area. There are special needs for Campground Host positions in the park's nine campgrounds.

Boone's Cave State Park

Agency: State parks
Season: Summer
Contact: Larry Hyde
49104 Morrow Mountain Rd.
Albemarle, NC 28001
E-mail: momo@vnet.net
Phone: (704) 982–4402

Description/Positions Available: This park, believed by some to have been the temporary home of Daniel Boone, features more than thirty species of wildflowers.

We need the following: a Natural Resource Interpreter, Maintenance Assistant, Park Attendant, and Trails Maintenance Worker.

Cape Lookout National Seashore

Agency: National Park Service
Season: Summer
Contact: Richard Meissner, Volunteer Coordinator
131 Charles St.
Harkers Island, NC 28531
E-mail: Richard_Meissner@nps.gov
Web: www.nps.gov/calo
Phone: (336) 728–2250

Description/Positions Available: We need Caretakers at Cape Lookout lighthouse and Portsmouth Village, a six-week or three-month commitment. Applicants must be CPR- and first-aid certified. Two persons (couples, friends) are required. Duties include light maintenance (cleaning buildings and toilets, cutting grass, etc.), meeting the public, and operating a small gift store. There is currently a waiting list. Folks with special talents are invited to contact us to see if their talent can be used (examples: computers, displays, naturalist, electrician, carpentry, clerical).

The park provides housing (sometimes shared with other volunteers) or RV hookups.

Contact one of the following: Cape Lookout Lighthouse Caretaker (current waiting list); Portsmouth Village Caretaker; Harkers Island Visitor Center (meeting the public, answering telephone, operating small gift store, etc).

Carl Sandburg National Historic Site

Agency: National Park Service
Season: Year-round
Contact: Jill Hamilton-Anderson
1928 Little River Rd.
Flat Rock, NC 28731
E-mail: Jill_Hamilton-Anderson@nps.gov
Web: www.nps.gov
Phone: (828) 693–4178

Description/Positions Available: Carl Sandburg

NHS is located in the village of Flat Rock. It is close to the Blue Ridge Parkway and Pisgah National Forest. Volunteers are needed to assist the staff with the historic dairy goat herd, education programs for adults and children, conducting house tours, and roving 240 acres with 5 miles of hiking trails. Carl Sandburg NHS honors a poet, historian, and humanitarian.

The following positions are available: Dairy Goat Farm Volunteer: care and feeding of small dairy herd, cheese making demonstrations, talk to visitors, assist staff with farm management; Trail Rovers: walk 5 miles of trails, trail maintenance, talk to visitors, assist staff with large groups of day use walkers; Tour Guide-Historic House: conduct tours, greet visitors, explain significance of Carl Sandburg, his works, and his life.

Carolina Beach State Park

Agency: State parks
Season: Year-round
Contact: Jeff Davis
P.O. Box 475
Carolina Beach, NC 24828
E-mail: carolina.beach@ncmail.net
Phone: (910) 458–8206

Description/Positions Available: Located 15 miles south of Wilmington, this park has a marina with forty-two boat slips and two launching ramps, eighty-three family campsites, two group camping areas, a picnic area, a visitor center with environmental education exhibits, and 6 miles of hiking trails. There are thirteen different natural plant communities, making it one of the most biologically diverse parks in North Carolina. The park's acidic, mineral-poor soil is home to the famous Venus flytrap and four other carnivorous plants that thrive by trapping and digesting insects.

A Campground Host is needed for the park campground. This post requires working weekends, holidays, and evening hours. You will be given a free campsite. A History Researcher is also necessary to research and write the history of the park. Other volunteer roles available include Trails Maintenance Worker and Maintenance Assistant.

Crowders Mountain State Park

Agency: State parks
Season: Year-round
Contact: Tim Dorsey
522 Park Office Lane
Kings Mountain, NC 28086
Phone: (704) 853–5375

Description/Positions Available: Located within the ancient King's Mountain Belt, Crowders Mountain State Park is characterized by rugged peaks that abruptly rise more than 800 feet above the surrounding landscape.

Volunteer opportunities include trails maintenance workers, groundskeepers, biological inventory analysts, natural resource interpreters, and visitor information assistants.

Eno River State Park

Agency: State parks
Season: Year-round
Contact: Adrienne Wallace
6101 Cole Mill Rd.
Durham , NC 27705
E-mail: enoriver@gte.net
Web: www.ils.unc.edu/parkproject/visit/enri/home.html
Phone: (919) 383–1686

Description/Positions Available: Eno River State Park has more than 2,800 acres to enjoy the following activities: hiking (approximately 20 miles), fishing (approximately 15 miles of river), canoeing, kayaking, primitive camping, picnicking, bird-watching and much more. A satellite park, Occoneechee State Natural Area, is also managed and is approximately 124 acres in size with two small fishing ponds and 2 miles of trails.

Opportunities include: Naturalist, Natural Resource Manager, Trail Work, Water Quality Monitoring, Species Inventory, Invasive Exotic Plant Eradication.

Goose Creek State Park

Agency: State parks
Season: Summer
Contact: Scott Kershner, Park Superintendent
2190 Camp Leach Rd.
Washington, NC 27889
Phone: (252) 923–2191

Description/Positions Available: The park lies along the sandy beaches of the Pamlico River among stately oaks draped with Spanish moss. An Environmental Interpreter and Trails Manager are needed.

Hanging Rock State Park

Agency: State parks
Season: Summer
Contact: Volunteer Manager
P.O. Box 278
Danbury, NC 27016
Phone: (336) 593–8480

Description/Positions Available: Local attractions include a panoramic view, sparkling mountain streams, waterfalls, and cascades.

A Campground Host is needed to register campers, provide information, and explain rules. You will be expected to perform light maintenance work such as picking up litter, stocking toilet facilities, and selling firewood. The post involves working weekends, holidays, and evening hours. A free campsite is provided. We also need a Natural Resource Interpreter, Maintenance Mechanic, and Trail Maintenance Worker.

Jones Lake State Park

Agency: State parks
Season: March 15 to December 1
Contact: Jeff Corbett
113 Jones Lake Dr.
Elizabethtown, NC 28337
Phone: (910) 588–4550

Description/Positions Available: Surrounded

by huge old trees, this park is located in the southern coastal plains and offers a variety of recreational opportunities.

Campground Hosts are needed from March 15 to December 1 to serve as live-in hosts at the park campground. This involves working weekends, holidays, and evening hours. A free campsite is provided. Trail Maintenance Workers are also needed to trim overgrowth; remove fallen trees and debris from trails; construct and build trail boardwalks; and maintain treadway, steps and bridges. Finally, we are looking for a Controlled-Burn Volunteer and Assistant Naturalist. Internships may be available.

Morrow Mountain State Park

Agency: State parks
Season: Year-round
Contact: Larry Hyde, Park Ranger
49104 Morrow Mountain Rd.
Albemarle, NC 28001
E-mail: momo@vnet.net
Web: www.ncsparks.net
Phone: (704) 982–4402

Description/Positions Available: Morrow Mountain State Park is a 4,700-acre park located in the Uwharrie Mountain range, one of the oldest mountain ranges in the world. The park has 16 miles of hiking trails, 16 miles of bridle trails, 106 family campsites, four backpack campsites, four group campsites, a swimming pool, boat launch, canoe and rowboat rentals, a historic homesite from the 1800s, and two scenic picnic areas. Barracks style housing is available for volunteers who work twenty hours or more per week.

The following posts are available: Campground Host, Trails Volunteer, Interpretive Volunteer, Maintenance Volunteer.

Morrow Mountain State Park

Agency: State parks
Season: Summer

Contact: Larry Hyde
49104 Morrow Mountain Rd.
Albemarle, NC 28001
E-mail: momo@vnet.net
Phone: (704) 982–4402

Description/Positions Available: Located in the ancient Uwharrie Mountains, this 4,700 acre park features family and group camping, cabins, a swimming pool, boat ramp, lake fishing, and 31 miles of trails.

We need a Kron House Interpreter to provide a living history interpretation to a 1800s homesite. A Campground Host is needed between March and October to assist in a 106-site campground (campsite with hookups provided). Also needed are Office Assistant, Trail Maintenance Worker, Park Attendant, Maintenance Assistant, Ornithologist and Seasonal Interpreter. Barracks housing is available for those who volunteer an average of twenty hours per week.

National Forests in North Carolina

Agency: U.S. Department of Agriculture Forest Service
Season: Year-round
Contact: J.C. Smith or Rebecca Allen
P.O. Box 2750
Asheville, NC 28805
E-mail: jsmith21@fs.fed.us
Web: www.cs.unca.edu/nfsnc/
Phone: (828) 257–4210 or (828) 257–4215

Description/Positions Available: There are four forests and three research areas in the state, with research facilities in South Carolina, Georgia, Virginia, and Florida, providing various opportunities from the mountains to the sea.

Pettigrew State Park

Agency: State parks
Season: Spring to fall
Contact: Sid Shearin, Superintendent
2252 Lake Shore Dr.

Creswell, NC 27928
Phone: (252) 797–4475

Description/Positions Available: This park is located along the shore of Lake Phelps, a 16,600-acre paradise for anglers, sailboaters, and windsurfers. Somerset Place, a state historic site, is also in the park. There are hiking and bicycle trails, a campground, fishing piers, and programs.

A Campground Host is needed to serve as live-in host at the park campground. This involves working weekends, holidays, and evening hours. A free campsite is provided. We are also recruiting a Natural Resource Interpreter to lead specialized programs, nature hikes, and evening programs. Finally, we need a Bird Specialist, a Receptionist, and an Astronomy Interpreter.

Pilot Mountain State Park

Agency: State parks
Season: Year-round
Contact: Keith Martin
1792 Pilot Knob Park Rd.
Pinnacle, NC 27043
Phone: (336) 325–2355

Description/Positions Available: Named for a large quartzite formation that rises 1,500 feet above its surroundings, this park is divided into two sections connected by a five-mile, 300-foot-wide corridor for hiking and horseback riding.

A Campground Host is needed to answer questions, perform light custodial work, clean and stock restrooms, sell firewood, and alert park staff to maintenance and security problems and camper emergencies. There are no electric hookups. We also need Park Attendants and an Assistant Maintenance Mechanic.

South Mountains State Park

Agency: State parks
Season: Summer
Contact: Superintendent

3001 South Mountains Park Ave.
Connelly Springs, NC 28612
E-mail: Southmountains@conninc.com
Phone: (828) 433–4772

Description/Positions Available: This park features High Shoals Waterfall, which tumbles 80 feet into a mountain stream.

A Trail Maintenance Worker is needed to help park staff trim overgrowth; remove fallen trees and debris from the trail path; construct and maintain erosion-control waterbars and berms; and maintain treadway, steps, and bridges. Please understand this is a voluntary position only (not a paid position)!

USDA Forest Service

Agency: U.S. Department of Agriculture Forest Service
Season: Year-round

Contact: Volunteer Program National Forests in North Carolina
P.O. Box 2750
Asheville, NC 28802
E-mail: jsmith21@fs.fed.us
Phone: (828) 257–4210 or (828) 257–4215

Description/Positions Available: You will be based at the national forests in North Carolina Southern Research Station. These forests offer volunteer programs to suit the needs of any person or group with the desire to assist in conservation or research. There are four national forests and three research areas in the state, with research facilities in South Carolina, Georgia, Mississippi, Alabama, Texas, Virginia, Louisiana, and Arkansas. Please contact the Volunteer Program National Forests in North Carolina.

Various volunteer opportunities are available.

North Dakota

Arrowwood National Wildlife Refuge

Agency: U.S. Fish and Wildlife Service
Season: Summer
Contact: Mark Vaniman
7745 11th St. S.E.
Pingree, ND 58476
E-mail: r6rw_arr@fws.gov
Web: www.r6.fws.gov/arrowwood/arwframes.html

Description/Positions Available: Thirty miles north of Jamestown. A Biological Aide is needed.

National Park Service/Amtrak

Agency: National Park Service
Season: Summer

Contact: Mike Casler
15550 Hwy. 1804
Williston, ND 58801
E-mail: Mike_Casler@nps.gov
Phone: (701) 572–9083

Description/Positions Available: See description under Nationwide listings in the front of this directory.

This program is presented on board Amtrak's "Empire Builder" between Minot, North Dakota, and Malta, Montana. We need Trails & Rails volunteers to ride once a month between these two cities. There are no housing, camping, or lodging facilities provided by the program. The only expenses covered are those associated with the actual program.

Oklahoma

National Park Service/Amtrak

Agency: National Park Service
Season: Summer
Contact: Susie Staples
P.O. Box 201
Sulphur, OK 73086
E-mail: Susie_Staples@nps.gov
Phone: (580) 622–3161, extension 205

Description/Positions Available: See description under Nationwide listings in the front of this directory.

This program is presented on board Amtrak's "Heartland Flyer" between Oklahoma City, Oklahoma, and Fort Worth, Texas. We need Trails & Rails volunteers to ride once a month between these two cities. There are no housing, camping or lodging facilities provided by the program. The only expenses covered are those associated with the actual program.

Oregon

Bureau of Land Management, Coos Bay District, Umpqua Resource Area

Agency: Bureau of Land Management
Season: Year-round
Contact: Larry Johnston
1300 Airport Lane
North Bend, OR 97459
E-mail: coos_bay@or.blm.gov
Web: www.or.blm.gov/coosbay/

Description/Positions Available: An Interpretive Natural Resources Intern/Volunteer is needed at the Umpqua Discovery Center (UDC) in Reedsport. This center interprets the natural and cultural history of the local area. Duties include developing educational programs; creating, setting up and maintaining displays; conducting group tours; staffing the gift shop; serving as a visitor contact; and possibly performing some site maintenance. Volunteers should be self-motivated and possess an interest in the environment, communications, or educational interpretation. Personal transportation and valid driver's license required. Benefits include housing, a stipend, mileage while on duty, a Bureau of Land Management uniform, and an opportunity to experience the beautiful southern Oregon coast.

We also need a Campground Host for the Dean Creek Elk Viewing Area, a 1,095-acre area along the Umpqua River (3 miles east of Reedsport), which features an open-air interpretive center, two vault toilets and flush restrooms, and two paved viewing areas with scopes. Duties include general site maintenance, such as emptying trashcans, mowing grass, cleaning restrooms, and collecting litter. Benefits include free trailer space and utilities, a stipend, and a Bureau of Land Management uniform. A pickup truck and valid driver's license are required.

Bureau of Land Management, Lakeview District, Klamath Falls Resource Area

Agency: Bureau of Land Management
Season: Spring to early fall
Contact: Scott Senter
2795 Anderson Ave., Bldg. 25
Klamath Falls, OR 97603
E-mail: Scott_Senter@or.blm.gov
Web: www.or.blm.gov/Lakeview/

Description/Positions Available: Located in the scenic Klamath Basin east of the Cascade Mountains in southern Oregon, this area offers excellent recreational opportunities, including fishing, camping, hunting, whitewater rafting, hiking, skiing, and mountain biking.

We require a Campground Host between June and September. Applicants must be friendly, helpful to the public, and able to perform minor maintenance. Bring your own trailer or RV. Two campgrounds with full hookups (power, water, and dump station) offer excellent fishing and scenery. A free campsite is provided. A River Ranger (recreation assistant) is also needed between May and September (flexible) on the Upper Klamath River to monitor the rafting-launch area, provide visitor assistance, drive a shuttle, perform light maintenance, and patrol the river. Possible housing and reimbursement for food and travel are available. A valid driver's license is required.

Bureau of Land Management, Roseburg District

Agency: Bureau of Land Management
Season: Year-round
Contact: Joe Ross, Multi-Resource Specialist
777 NW Garden Valley Blvd.
Roseburg, OR 97470
E-mail: Joseph_Ross@or.blm.gov
Web: www.or.blm.gov/roseburg/
Phone: (541) 440–4930

Description/Positions Available: We operate programs on 425,000 acres of public land within Douglas County, Oregon.

Volunteers are required to host in campgrounds, maintain trails, reclaim mined lands, construct fences, paint buildings and assist with in-office tasks such as data input. We attempt to find a place for all volunteers who contact us with an expression of interest. We also host interns and crews through such programs as Apprenticeships in Science and Engineering (ASE), Resource Apprentice Program for Students (RAPS), U.S. Dept. of Interior Minority Intern Program,

Northwest Youth Corps, Oregon Youth Conservation Corps, and other partnerships. National Public Lands Day is an annual event in September that attracts a large number of volunteers for various projects.

Bureau of Land Management, Salem District

Agency: Bureau of Land Management
Season: Year-round, but primarily summer
Contact: J. Grant
P.O. Box 785
Mill City, OR 97360
E-mail: jgrant@or.blm.gov
Web: www.or.blm.gov/salem/
Phone: (503) 897–2406

Description/Positions Available: This district is located within ninety minutes of the Pacific Northwest's many attractions. From oceans to mountains, large cities to wilderness, lakes and rivers to desert areas, this area offers a variety of terrain and recreational opportunities.

Park Aides are needed for a combination of maintenance, public contact, trail work, and administrative duties. Benefits include housing, a weekly subsistence of $100 per week, work insurance, and training. Positions are available in all seasons, with summer being the priority. The length of appointments is negotiable, but we prefer a minimum commitment of 12 weeks. Those wanting summer positions should contact the Bureau of Land Management before May. Campground Hosts are needed April through October for many attractive sites. Duties include light maintenance and public relations. Benefits include the provision of a site with utilities, liability and work-injury insurance and a subsistence of $25 per week. A River Corridor Host is also needed between July and Labor Day. Duties include patrolling a 12-mile stretch of wild and scenic river corridor, providing public contact, light maintenance, and assistance to the nearby Campground Host. Benefits include the provision of a site with utilities, liability and work-injury insurance, and a subsistence of $25 per week. A vehicle for patrolling may be provided if funding is available. Finally, Maintenance Campers are needed for regularly scheduled maintenance tasks. These may include: janitorial, grounds, building, and facility-type work. Benefits include the provision of a campsite with utilities, liability and work-injury insurance, and a negotiable weekly subsistence (dependent on hours worked and schedule).

Deschutes National Forest

Agency: U.S. Department of Agriculture Forest Service
Season: Spring to fall
Contact: Linda Lee
P.O. Box 208
Crescent, OR 97733
Phone: (541) 433–3206, extension 2234

Description/Positions Available: Crescent is located in Central Oregon's High Desert, consisting of the Cascade Mountains and high elevation lakes, streams, meadows, and forests.

We offer a wide array of volunteer opportunities, including projects in recreation, forestry, botany, fisheries, wildlife, cultural resources, trail maintenance, visitor services, computer input, and more. Depending on the position, subsistence stipends, housing and full hookup RV sites may be available.

Fremont National Forest, Bly District

Agency: U.S. Department of Agriculture Forest Service
Season: Spring to fall
Contact: Steve Cornell
P.O. Box 25
Bly, OR 97622
Phone: (541) 353–2751

Description/Positions Available: Featuring the Gearhart Mountain Wilderness, this district is located between Klamath Falls and Lakeview and offers a chance to enjoy excellent wildlife

viewing, fishing, and clean air.

A Campground Host is needed to assist campers, maintain campgrounds, and collect information. Applicants must have access to their own camper. No hookups are available. Wilderness Guards are also being recruited. Duties include greeting users, conducting tours, maintaining trails, and collecting data. A Recreation Technician is needed to clean and maintain campgrounds and trails, including painting and repairing structures. Possible housing and subsistence are available.

Fremont National Forest, Lakeview District

Agency: U.S. Department of Agriculture Forest Service
Season: Summer
Contact: Larry Hills
HC 64, Box 60
Lakeview, OR 97630
Phone: (541) 947–6275

Description/Positions Available: Considered the hang-gliding capital of the West, this area in southeastern Oregon offers a wonderful mixture of forests and high desert.

A Recreation Assistant is needed to maintain recreation areas, take user counts, perform minor carpentry work, and maintain trail systems.

John Day Fossil Beds National Monument

Agency: National Park Service
Season: Year-round
Contact: John Fiedor
HCR 82, Box 126
Kimberly, OR 97848
E-mail: joda_interpretation@nps.gov
Web: www.nps.gov/joda
Phone: (541) 987–2333

Description/Positions Available: The landscape of John Day Fossil Beds, in the Blue

Mountains of eastern Oregon, is typical near-desert grassland-sagebrush-juniper country in the lowlands, and ponderosa pine forests on the mountain ridges. It has a population density of less than two people per square mile, and has remarkably diverse recreational opportunities. John Day Fossil Beds National Monument has two perennial volunteer positions available. The Winter Caretaker position runs from November into March and is located at the Painted Hills Unit of the monument. A furnished residence is provided for the caretaker, who tends to perform routine maintenance of the 3,000-acre unit, patrols the unit by vehicle and hikes, and contacts and greets visitors. A single volunteer or couple is desired for this four-month position. Some reimbursement is available. A second volunteer position runs from spring into fall. For this position, each volunteer's tenure will last from one to three months, as negotiated. This Visitor Center Aide position involves helping staff the Sheep Rock Unit's fossil museum and assisting visitors with their trip through the park. Weekly trail hikes are also conducted on this unit's 5 miles of trails to help check on conditions, greet visitors, and note needed repairs. A knowledge and interest in geology is desired. A trailer pad with full hookups is provided on a nearby Bureau of Land Management site for the volunteer to provide his or her own residence. Volunteers need their own vehicle for the 10-mile commute to the park. Again, some reimbursement is available. Responses to questions on these positions can be sought by contacting the park at joda_interpretation@nps.gov.

The Painted Hills Unit Winter Caretaker position is available for an individual or couple. This volunteer position runs between November and mid-March of each year. Please apply before September of each year. The Sheep Rock Visitor Center Aide position runs from spring to fall, one volunteer position is available for an individual or couple, and tenure may be negotiated for one to three months. The application period runs from January to August of each year.

Mount Hood National Forest

Agency: U.S. Department of Agriculture Forest Service
Season: Summer
Contact: Shelley Butler
70220 E. Hwy. 26
Zigzag, OR 97049
E-mail: sebutler@fs.fed.us
Web: www.fs.fed.us/r6/mthood/

Description/Positions Available: Wilderness Guards (two); Interpretive specialists—Timberline Lodge (three); Trail maintenance and construction (four); and Wilderness Stewards (three) for Mount Hood and Bull of the Woods Wilderness.

Mount Hood National Forest, Zigzag Rd

Agency: U.S. Department of Agriculture Forest Service
Season: Year-round
Contact: Kathleen Walker
70220 E. Hwy. 26
Zigzag, OR 97055
E-mail: kwalker@fs.fed.us
Web: www.fs.fed.us/r6/mthood
Phone: (503) 622–3191

Description/Positions Available: Zigzag Ranger District is one hour (50 miles) east of Portland.

We are looking for Wilderness Stewards and Interpretive Volunteers. Housing is available for full-time volunteers. Volunteer stipends for expenses are also available. Duties for full- and part-time Wilderness Stewards include working between Thursday and Monday. Weekends will usually be camped out in the backcountry (high-use wilderness destinations). Stewards will make visitor contacts, collect data, and assist in wilderness restoration and trail maintenance. Training, travel and some equipment are provided. You must have some backpacking experience. Opportunities exist between May and October.

We prefer a three-month commitment for full-time volunteers. Contact Kathleen Walker (ext. 641) or Mary Ellen Fitzgerald (ext. 625) for more information. We also offer opportunities to Interpretive Volunteers for the Historic Timberline Lodge, which attracts more than one million annual visitors. Duties include providing lodge tours, nature walks, campfire programs, and staffing the information desk. Training and transportation are provided. These positions are available all year-round. We prefer a three-month commitment. Contact Michelle Franulovich (ext. 610).

Newberry National Volcanic Monument

Agency: U.S. Department of Agriculture Forest Service
Season: Year-round
Contact: Keith Clinton
1230 N.E. 3rd St., Suite A262
Bend, OR 97701
E-mail: kclinton@fs.fed.us
Web: www.fs.fed.us/r6/centraloregon
Phone: (541) 383–4790

Description/Positions Available: The Newberry National Volcanic Monument is an outstanding feature of the Deschutes National Forest. Lying just east of the Cascade Mountains in beautiful central Oregon, the area is relatively dry and has blue skies, warm summer days, cool nights, and crisp snowy winters. Elevation ranges from 3,500 feet in town to 10,000 feet on the mountaintops. There are numerous mountains, lakes, streams, and trails to explore. Volunteer opportunities are available both summer and winter.

There is always a need for volunteer Interpretive Naturalists to work with paid staff educating and assisting the public. We are especially interested in finding volunteers who are experienced educators. Winter sites include Mount Bachelor Ski and Summer Resort and Lava Lands Visitor Center. Summer sites include Mount Bachelor, Lava Lands, Historic Elk Lake Guard Station, Lava River Cave (a large lava tube, 1 mile long), and others.

Oregon Caves National Monument

Agency: National Park Service
Season: Year-round
Contact: Roger Brandt
19000 Caves Hwy.
Cave Junction, OR 97523
E-mail: roger_brandt@nps.gov
Web: www.nps.gov/orca
Phone: (541) 592–2100, extension 225

Description/Positions Available: This monument is located in the Siskiyou Mountains of southwestern Oregon, an area characterized by unusual geology, deep forests, and scenic rivers. The monument has three wilderness areas located nearby. Smith River National Recreation Area, Redwood National Park, Crater Lake National Park and the scenic Oregon Coast are all within a couple of hours drive of the monument. Temperatures in the summer are commonly in the lower nineties with cool nights. Spring and fall have cool temperatures with some rain. Winters commonly bring between one and four feet of snow to the headquarters area. Upper elevations offer great snowshoeing. The monument has a three-mile cave system that contains decorated passageways; a population of cave adapted life; ice age fossils; and a small population of bats. A small stream comes out of the cave and flows into the Rogue River watershed well known for its runs of salmon and steelhead. Above the cave is an old growth forest of Port Orford cedar, Douglas fir and a fern-covered forest floor. A 2-mile hike above the monument will take you to the Bigelow Lakes nestled in a small, alpine glacial cirque. Vistas from the top look into the Red Buttes wilderness, Marble Mountains wilderness and Siskiyou Wilderness. Visitors to the monument take cave tours, hike short loop trails, or walk through the Oregon Caves Chateau, a structure on the National Register of Historic Landmarks. Children participate in the Junior Ranger Program or do Trail Activity sheets to earn badges and buttons. During spring and fall months, the monument schedules school groups for the Environmental Education Program, which qualifies them to have an activity pack sent to their class as well as a Ranger-conducted program in class, a free cave tour, and a nature walk through the forest conducted by one of the staff. The monument has two trailer sites with full hookups (excepting phone services). There may be housing available in the historic chalet for individuals needing a place to stay. The monument pays for all housing and utilities as well as offering a small stipend to cover expenses.

We need Visitor Center Staff (spring, summer or fall) to work in an information station or visitor center directing visitors to various attractions or telling them about cave tours. Work may also involve children as part of the monument's Junior Ranger Program. Collateral duties might include assignments to develop handouts, brochures, trail guides, etc. Training and orientation will help staff become familiar with local resources as well as with resources in the local region (an area encompassing the Redwood coast and the Cascade Mountains). Trail roves, conducting nature walks, or delivering short public programs may also be part of the job depending upon the interest of the individual volunteer.

Cave Guides are needed (spring, summer, or fall) to conduct cave tours through the caves. Tours cover approximately a half-mile with climbing, stooping and ducking an integral part of the job. The job requires staff to become familiar with the resources and processes of the cave (cave formation, cave-adapted life, natural cave winds, ice age fossils, the impacts of forest fire on the cave environment, water resources, geologic history). Much of this will be covered in training and handouts to be given to staff. Trail roves, conducting nature walks, or delivering short public programs may also be part of the job depending upon the interest of the individual volunteer.

Environmental Education staff (fall or spring)

will be employed to conduct environmental education programs for visiting schools. Duties include conducting cave tours, forest walks, and occasional rainy day programs. Training will cover how to deliver cave tours and nature walks as well as give staff an opportunity to observe several programs before they begin leading groups on their own. Any combination of the above opportunities will also be considered. We work with staff to give them as many opportunities for having a diversified experience at Oregon Caves National Monument. We also try to schedule staff into other departments that have projects that capture their interest. This might include assisting with cave restoration work, development of handicap accessible trails, research, etc.

Oregon Parks and Recreation, Columbia Gorge District, Friends of Vista House

Agency: State parks
Season: Year-round
Contact: Executive Director
P.O. Box 204
Corbett, OR 97019
Phone: (503) 695–2230

Description/Positions Available: Volunteers are needed to staff the information desk, dispensing interpretive information to the nearly one million annual visitors. We also have an immediate opening for an Interpretive Specialist. Benefits include interpretive volunteer training, a one-day bus training familiarization tour, a cruise on the sternwheeler, excursion to Mount Hood RR, plus a banquet to honor volunteers at the end of the season. Folk Artists are needed for the popular volunteer Folk Art Program.

Siskiyou National Forest, Two Rivers Zone

Agency: U.S. Department of Agriculture Forest Service
Season: Summer

Contact: Judith McHugh
200 N.E. Greenfield Rd.
Grants Pass, OR 97528
E-mail: jmchugh@fs.fed.us
Phone: (541) 592–4000

Description/Positions Available: Located in Southern Oregon, the Siskiyou National Forest has five locations available for Camp Hosts. All locations are rustic campgrounds with no electricity, no RV sewer hookups, or flush toilets. The sites offer solitude, running streams, vault toilets, and friendly visitors. One campground has a lake, another a small pond.

This position compensates the volunteer with $10 per diem, propane for heating and cooking, and official use of a personally owned cell phone. Reimbursement for other expenses can be negotiated. Volunteers spend their days welcoming visitors, re-stocking paper in the restrooms, and enjoying the beautiful Southern Oregon summer. Most camp hosts prefer to have their own RV or similar accommodations.

Siskiyou National Forest, Two Rivers Zone

Agency: U.S. Department of Agriculture Forest Service
Season: Summer
Contact: Judith McHugh
200 N.E. Greenfield Rd.
Grants Pass, OR 97528
E-mail: jmchugh@fs.fed.us
Phone: (541) 592–4000

Description/Positions Available: Located in Southern Oregon, the Siskiyou National Forest is seeking volunteers to work with our recreation crews. The volunteers will perform a variety of physical tasks including trail maintenance and construction, campground maintenance and assisting during Forest patrol days. Physical fitness, sturdy work boots with 8-inch tops and Vibram soles, and an ability to work in temperatures ranging from sixty-five to 105 degrees are required.

This position compensates the volunteer with $10 per diem, and all tools required for the work. Reimbursement for other expenses can be negotiated. Government housing may be available.

Siskiyou National Forest, Two Rivers Zone

Agency: U.S. Department of Agriculture Forest Service
Season: Winter
Contact: Judith McHugh
200 N.E. Greenfield Rd.
Grants Pass, OR 97528
E-mail: jmchugh@fs.fed.us
Phone: (541) 592–4000

Description/Positions Available: Located in Southern Oregon, the Page Mountain Snow-Park provides winter recreation opportunities for nearby communities. The Snow-Park is open November 15 to April 15 each year. We are upgrading the host facility to provide electricity, possibly water, and shelter for an RV. The park has a vault toilet and two snow huts. The park is part of the Statewide Snow-Park program and receives extensive use by sledders, cross-country skiers, snow-boarders and the occasional snowmobiler.

This position compensates the volunteer with $10 per diem, propane for heating and cooking, and official use of a personally owned cell phone. Reimbursement for other expenses can be negotiated.

Siuslaw National Forest, South Zone Public Affairs

Agency: U.S. Department of Agriculture Forest Service
Season: Year-round
Contact: John Zapell
4480 Hwy. 101N, Bldg. G
Florence, OR 97439
E-mail: jzapell@fs.fed.us
Web: www.fs.fed.us/r6/siuslaw/oregondunes

Phone: (541) 902–6976

Description/Positions Available: Breathtaking sand dunes stretch 42 miles along the coast from Florence to Coos Bay. The National Recreation Area attracts one-and-a-half-million visitors annually due to the variety of recreation opportunities. Enjoy hiking, boating, fishing, birding, or motorized recreation within these sand dunes. Dense, temperate rainforests give way to a sea of sand, seasonal wetlands, thirty coastal lakes, estuaries, and pristine ocean beaches.

Volunteers are needed to work in Public Affairs, Trail Management, Wildlife Management, Campground Recreation and Maintenance, Office Support, and Visitor Center Services. Volunteers are expected to work five days per week. Training, housing, uniform, basic equipment and a stipend of $12 per diem are provided. Applicant must posses good communication skills, be willing to work with the public, work in inclement weather, and provide own foul-weather gear and hiking boots. Positions typically begin in March and last into October. There is a minimum tour of 90 days. This position can be used to fulfill school internship or project requirements. We currently need interpreters, naturalists, trail crew workers, ATV assistants, visitor center staff, birders, biologists, and technicians. Please submit your resume and indicate which position interests you.

Siuslaw National Forest, Waldport–Cape Perpetua District

Agency: U.S. Department of Agriculture Forest Service
Season: Year-round
Contact: Kristine Cochrane
P.O. Box 274
Yachats, OR 97498
Phone: (541) 547–3289

Description/Positions Available: The spectacular Cape Perpetua Scenic Area, located on the central coast, is home to abundant marine and land wildlife. The area also features tide pools, ancient spruce forests, rocky coastal headlands, and migrating gray whales.

A Naturalist is needed to conduct guided nature walks twice a day, conduct weekend campfire programs, and fill in at the front-desk area. Subsistence and limited housing are available.

Wallowa-Whitman National Forest

Agency: U.S. Department of Agriculture Forest Service
Season: Summer
Contact: Tom Carlson
88401 Hwy. 82
Enterprise, OR 97828
E-mail: tcarlson@fs.fed.us
Web: www.fs.fed.us/r6/w-w/
Phone: (541) 426–5536

Description/Positions Available: Eagle Cap Wilderness, Enterprise, Oregon. The Eagle Cap Wilderness is the largest wilderness in Oregon (365,000 acres) and is located in the scenic Blue Mountains of northeastern Oregon. The topography ranges from long forested valleys at 3,000 feet elevation to high alpine lakes at 7,000 and snow-capped peaks at nearly 10,000 feet. The area is popular for both hikers and recreation livestock users during the late June through September season.

We require a Wilderness Ranger. Duties for this position include contacting visitors to pass along information on wilderness regulations and zero-impact techniques, campsite cleanup and litter removal, campsite inventory, and restoration and revegetation of campsites and nonsystem trail segments. The volunteer will backpack or use horses to access the wilderness for ten days at a time with four days off before the next tour. Training is provided in wilderness management and ethics, zero-impact techniques, public contact, restoration, inventory, first aid, CPR, and fire fighting (if desired). A bunkhouse is available at no cost near Wallowa Lake for off-day housing. A subsistence of $15 per diem will be paid for each day worked. The position requires strenuous physical activity, a basic knowledge of backcountry travel and camping, an interest in wilderness management, and a willingness to talk with a variety of people about their wilderness experience. A personal vehicle is not required for work but is strongly recommended for off-duty purposes. Flexible dates between mid-June and mid-September are available.

Pennsylvania

Black Moshannon State Park

Agency: State parks
Season: Spring to fall
Contact: Park Manager
4216 Beaver Rd.
Philipsburg, PA 16866
Phone: (814) 342–5960

Description/Positions Available: This park, located near a 250-acre lake, is almost surrounded by bog and other wetlands. There are excellent opportunities to observe a wide variety of wildlife.

Currently, we need Trail Maintenance and Construction Workers.

Clear Creek State Park

Agency: State parks
Season: Summer
Contact: Greg Burkett
RR #1, Box 82
Sigel, PA 15860
E-mail: clearcreek@dcnr.state.pa.us
Web: www.dcnr.state.pa.us/stateparks/parks/clear.htm

Description/Positions Available: Clear Creek State Park is located in Northwestern Pennsylvania along the Clarion River. It has 1,676 mostly wooded acres and 20 miles of hiking trails, as well as camping and rustic cabins.

The park needs volunteers to maintain trails and to serve as Campground Hosts.

Delaware Water Gap National Recreation Area

Agency: National Park Service
Season: Year-round
Contact: Megan O'Malley
Delaware Water Gap NRA
Bushkill, PA 18324
E-mail: Megan_O'Malley@nps.gov
Web: www.nps.gov/dewa
Phone: (908) 496–4458

Description/Positions Available: Delaware Water Gap National Recreation Area is a unit of the National Park System that encompasses approximately 70,000 acres along the Delaware River in Pennsylvania and New Jersey.

Volunteers are needed in a variety of positions in the park. For more details please visit our Web site or the National Park Service Web site at www.nps.gov/volunteers.

Erie National Wildlife Refuge

Agency: U.S. Fish and Wildlife Service
Season: March to October
Contact: Jeff Hass
11296 Wood Duck Lane
Guys Mills, PA 16327
E-mail: Jeff_Hass@fws.gov
Web: erie.fws.gov

Description/Positions Available: This 8,777-acre refuge features beaver ponds, pools and marshland, bounded by forested slopes that support croplands, grasslands and wet meadows. The refuge is a haven for migratory birds such as bald eagles, herons, wood ducks, and

Canada geese. The headquarters/visitor center is 10 miles east of Meadville on the outskirts of Guys Mills village.

An Interpreter is needed to staff the visitor center and conduct programs. Maintenance Workers are needed for building, grounds and trail upkeep. We are also looking for a Biologist to help with visitor surveys and data collection. Our current needs in all of these areas are for the period between March and October.

Fort Necessity National Battlefield

Agency: National Park Service
Season: Year-round
Contact: Carney Rigg, Volunteer Coordinator
1 Washington Pkwy.
Farmington, PA 15437
E-mail: carney_rigg@nps.gov
Web: www.nps.gov/fone/

Description/Positions Available: We are located in southwestern Pennsylvania, 60 miles southeast of Pittsburgh, Pennsylvania.

We are in need of Interpreters for the French and Indian War site; living history soldiers; guides for the 1828 National Road tavern, and Visitor Center use assistants.

Greenwood Furnace State Park

Agency: National Park Service
Season: Year-round
Contact: Genny Volgstadt
RR 2, Box 118
Huntingdon, PA 16652
E-mail: greenwoodfurnace@state.pa.us
Web: www.dcnr.state.pa.ua
Phone: (814) 667–1800

Description/Positions Available: We are located in Central Pennsylvania, thirty minutes south of State College on Route 305.

Opportunities are offered in the following areas: Trail Maintenance, internships in park management or interpretation.

Hopewell Furnace National Historic Site

Season: Year-round
Agency: National Park Service
Contact: Frank Hebblethwaite
2 Mark Bird Lane
Elverson, PA 19520
E-mail: hofu_superintendent@nps.gov
Web: www.nps.gov/hofu
Phone: (610) 582–8773

Description/Positions Available: Located in southeastern Pennsylvania, just 15 miles from Reading (the "outlet capital of the world") and 45 miles west of Philadelphia but still in a very rural area. It is surrounded on three sides by the 7,500-acre French Creek State Park and is close to Pennsylvania Dutch Country.

A position is available for a Curatorial Assistant. The Curatorial Assistant obtains an overview of collection management by assisting the Park Ranger (Cultural Resources) with historic housekeeping, library work, reorganization of storage, environmental monitoring, accessioning, and cataloging. Individual projects are assigned based on the changing needs of the park. Archival projects are currently a priority.

A Volunteer Interpreter is also needed. In the summer this involves portraying a Hopewell resident from the 1830s through the technique of living history. This may include molding and casting demonstrations, demonstrations of domestic crafts, brick oven baking, blacksmithing, farming, or charcoal making. During the fall or the spring a Volunteer Interpreter would be involved in giving tours to school groups. Some interns have also performed clerical work and staffed the visitor center information desk.

Natural Resources Assistants are required. Candidates should be pursuing a career in natural science, land management, or a related field. Duties include various projects associated with managing the natural resources of an 848-acre historic site. This includes vegetation monitoring, computer data entry, Geographic Information

System development, mapping, wildlife inventory and monitoring, and exotic vegetation control.

Maintenance Assistants are also being recruited. Interns work with tradespeople (Wood Crafter, Maintenance Mechanic, etc.) performing duties such as painting, repairing historic structures, and splitting wood for charcoal burns. These duties also involve working with the facility manager on inventories, condition assessments, and administrative functions. Maintenance Assistants gain first-hand knowledge about the day-to-day operations of a National Park Service Historic Site and the maintenance of historic structures.

Independence National Historical Park

Agency: National Park Service
Season: Year-round
Contact: Steve Sitarski
313 Walnut St.
Philadelphia, PA 19106
E-mail: antoinette_jett@nps.gov
Web: www.nps.gov/inde
Phone: (215) 597–1293

Description/Positions Available: Independence National Historical Park is located in downtown Philadelphia and is often referred to as the birthplace of our nation. At the park, you can see the Liberty Bell and Independence Hall. In addition, the park interprets the events and the lives of the diverse population during the years when Philadelphia was the capital of the United States (from 1790 to 1800).

We have volunteer opportunities in the following areas: Guide Office Clerk, Gardener Researcher Archivist, Computer Assistant, Seamstress, Alarm Technician, Architectural Technician, Group Projects.

John Heinz National Wildlife Refuge at Tinicum

Agency: U.S. Fish and Wildlife Service

Season: Year Round
Contact: Cyrus Brame
2 International Plaza, Suite 104
Philadelphia, PA 19113
E-mail: cyrus_brame@fws.gov
Phone: (215) 365–3118

Description/Positions Available: Containing the largest remaining freshwater tidal marsh in Pennsylvania, this park is also home to a wide variety of plants and animals typical of a wetland environment. The center's primary objective is to provide people with environmental education opportunities.

An Interpreter is needed to lead family nature programs. Maintenance Workers are needed for buildings, grounds, and trail work. Finally, an Educator is needed to help with environmental-education programs.

Kings Gap Environmental Ed Center

Agency: State parks
Season: Year-round
Contact: Volunteer Coordinator
500 Kings Gap Rd.
Carlisle, PA 17013
E-mail: kingsgapsp@state.pa.us
Web: www.dcnr.state.pa.us
Phone: (717) 486–5031

Description/Positions Available: Located a mile east of the Huntsdale Fish Hatchery, this facility features varied topography and scenic features and overlooks, and its pine plantation makes for excellent hiking. Kings Gap also provides an orienteering course.

Volunteer needed to assist with maintenance of trails, grounds, and buildings. A Clerical Assistant is needed to help with mailings, typing, filing, phone calls, and visitor questions. An Environmental Education Assistant is also needed to teach various age groups on requested environmental topics. Benefits include training, worker's compensation, and the satisfaction of helping your community in a spectacular natural environment.

Ohiopyle State Park

Agency: State parks
Season: Year-round
Contact: Daniel K. Bickel
P.O. Box 105
Ohiopyle, PA 15470
E-mail: ohiopyle@dncr.state.pa.us
Web: www.dcnr.state.pa.us
Phone: (724) 329–8591

Description/Positions Available: Southwestern Pennsylvania. Take State Route 381 south through the Borough of Ohiopyle; the Park Office is located on Dinnerbell Road just off Route 381.

Current opportunities include: Invasive Species Control, Bicycle Patrol, River Patrol, Trail Maintenance, Campground Hosting.

Park Dam State Park

Agency: State parks
Season: Spring to fall
Contact: H. Scott Streator
R.d. 1, Box 165
Penfield, PA 15849
Phone: (814) 765–0630

Description/Positions Available: Located in central Pennsylvania on the edge of a large wilderness area, this park features a twenty-acre lake, visitor center, interpretive center and other attractions.

Volunteers are needed to serve as Naturalist Aides and to help with maintenance, arts and crafts for kids, and Trail Maintenance. Camping fees can be waived in return for volunteer work.

Pennsylvania Bureau of State Parks and Bureau of Forestry

Agency: State parks
Season: Year-round
Contact: Jim Zambo

P.O. Box 8551
Harrisburg, PA 17101
E-mail: jzambo@state.pa.us
Web: dcnr.state.pa.us

Description/Positions Available: A park is within 25 miles of every citizen. There are 116 state parks throughout Pennsylvania with two million acres of state forest.

We are recruiting a Conservation Volunteer to work on a Trails and Wildlife Habitat project to create or clear hiking trails, improve wildlife habitat, and clean and stabilize stream banks. Interpretation/Environmental Education skills are also needed. Volunteers will interpret the interrelationships between people and their natural, cultural, and historic environments, and assist with visitor centers. Campground Hosts serve as model campers, who greet and assist other campers, and perform light maintenance. Your camping fee is waived and electricity provided. Maintenance Workers are also always needed to plant trees and flowers, repair foot bridges, improve accessibility, install park signs, and perform other light maintenance. If you are interested in researching and writing the history of forests and state parks, and/or developing checklists of flora and fauna, please get in touch. Other positions are available and can be tailored to your skills.

Pine Grove Furnace State Park

Agency: State parks
Season: Year-round
Contact: William Rosevear
1100 Pine Grove Rd.
Gardners, PA 17324
Phone: (717) 486–7174

Description/Positions Available: Located in the Michaux State Forest, this park is nestled in the mountains of the South Mountain range and includes two lakes. The park is recognized on the National Register of Historic Places for its significant charcoal and cast-iron industry and features many historic structures. The park provides a full range of recreational services, including camping, trout fishing, picnicking, and swimming as well as interpretive and environmental education programs.

Maintenance Workers, Campground Hosts, and Informational Aides are needed. Benefits include training, worker's compensation if injured, and free camping for hosts.

Pocono Environmental Education Center (PEEC)

Agency: NON PRO
Season: Year-round
Contact: Thomas E. Shimalla
RR 2, Box 1010
Dingmans Ferry, PA 18328
E-mail: Shimalla@peec.org
Web: www.peec.org
Phone: (610) 828–9281

Description/Positions Available: The Pocono Environmental Education Center (PEEC) is set on the Pocono Plateau in northeastern Pennsylvania within the 70,000-acre Delaware Water Gap National Recreation Area. The thirty-eight-acre campus is located between Stroudsburg and Milford, Pennsylvania, off Route 209 and is within easy driving distance of New York, New Jersey, Philadelphia, and Connecticut.

We have openings for Trail Crews, Landscapers, Carpenters, and Painters. Transportation to PEEC can be arranged from nearby towns that are accessible by public transportation. PEEC provides meals and accommodations in exchange for volunteer services.

Prince Gallitzin State Park

Agency: State parks
Season: Spring to fall
Contact: J. William Mansberger
966 Marina Rd.
Patton, PA 16668-6317
Phone: (814) 674–1000

Description/Positions Available: This park, situated in the scenic Allegheny Plateau region of Pennsylvania, offers a variety of outdoor recreation experiences, including hiking, fishing, picnicking, swimming, and camping amid mixed hardwood forests, and a 1,600-acre lake.

Volunteers are needed to assist in maintenance, environmental education and research, and information dissemination. Benefits include training and worker's compensation if injured.

Sizerville State Park

Agency: State parks
Season: Year-round
Contact: R. Dana Crisp or Sara M. Fowler
RR1, Box 238
Emporium, PA 15834
E-mail: sizerville@dcnr.state.pa.us
Web: dcnr.state.pa.us
Phone: (814) 486–5605

Description/Positions Available: We operate a 386-acre state park adjacent to Elk and Susquehannock State Forests. The park contains five trails that are in need of TLC and recommendations for improvement. These vary from easy to moderately difficult.

Volunteers for trail maintenance, possible trail development or relocation, and general input (i.e. its interest, difficulty, route, etc.) would be valuable to our enterprise.

Puerto Rico

Caribbean Islands National Wildlife Refuge

Agency: U.S. Fish and Wildlife Service
Season: Year-round
Contact: Joseph Schwagerl
P.O. Box 510
Boqueron, PR 00622

E-mail: Joseph_Schwagerl@fws.gov
Web: caribbean.fws.gov/index.html

Description/Positions Available: Volunteers are needed for: reforestation, trail maintenance, native tree nursery work, forest inventory, and more.

Rhode Island

John H. Chafee Blackstone River Valley National Heritage Corridor

Agency: National Park Service
Season: Year-round
Contact: Suzanne Buchanan, Ranger
One Depot Square
Woonsocket, RI 02895
E-mail: Suzanne_Buchanan@nps.gov
Web: nps.gov/blac
Phone: (401) 762–0440

Description/Positions Available: The John H. Chafee Blackstone River Valley National Heritage Corridor is a special type of national park. It is a region of 250,000 acres between Worcester, Massachusetts and Providence, Rhode Island. The National Heritage Corridor includes whole cities and towns, dozens of villages and a half million people. The federal government does not own or manage land as it does in more traditional national parks. Instead, people, businesses, nonprofit historic and environmental organizations, twenty-four local and two state governments, the National Park Service, and a unifying commission work together to protect its special identity and prepare for the valley's future. Volunteer opportunities are countless. Call for information on the VIP program and for a full list of current volunteer opportunities.

South Carolina

Congaree Swamp National Monument

Agency: National Park Service
Season: Year-round
Contact: Lewis G. Prettyman
100 National Park Rd.
Hopkins, SC 29061
E-mail: Lewis_Prettyman@nps.gov

Web: www.nps.gov/cosw
Phone: (803) 776–4396, extension 22

Description/Positions Available: Congaree Swamp National Monument is a rare 22,200-acre old-growth bottomland hardwood forest located approximately 20 miles southeast of Columbia, South Carolina. Columbia is within a two-hour drive of the coastal city of Charleston and within three hours of the Blue Ridge Mountains.

We offer opportunities in Visitor Services (Visitor Center Information), Front and Backcountry Maintenance, and Resource Management.

Congaree Swamp National Monument

Agency: National Park Service
Season: Year-round
Contact: Fran Rametta, Park Naturalist
100 National Park Rd.
Hopkins, SC 29061
Phone: (803) 776–4396, extension 11

Description/Positions Available: This wilderness area, located approximately 20 miles from Columbia, offers a wide variety of recreational opportunities.

Volunteers are needed for Interpretation, Maintenance and Resource Management. Immediate openings are available for positions such as Biology Aide, Interpretive Assistant, and Maintenance Technician. Opportunities in other fields are also available; contact us for our latest listings. Benefits may include trailer space.

Francis Marion National Forest

Agency: U.S. Department of Agriculture Forest Service
Season: Year-round
Contact: John Dupre
1015 Pinckney St.
Mcclellanville, SC 29458
E-mail: jdupre@fs.fed.us
Web: www.fs.fed.us/r8/fms/

Description/Positions Available: The Francis Marion National Forest is located in the coastal plain just north of the historic city of Charleston. Best outdoor working conditions are in the fall, winter, and early spring.

We need help with trail construction and maintenance, interpretation and education, and wildlife management.

Kings Mountain National Military Park

Agency: National Park Service
Season: Year-round
Contact: Chris Revels, Chief Ranger
2625 Park Rd.
Blacksburg, SC 29702
E-mail: chris_revels@nps.gov
Web: www.nps.gov/kimo
Phone: (864) 936–7921

Description/Positions Available: Kings Mountain National Military Park is located in the Piedmont Region of South Carolina between Spartanburg, South Carolina, and Charlotte, North Carolina. The park is composed of a mixed hardwood forest and traverses rolling hills typical of the Piedmont Region. Summers are hot and humid. Winters are generally mild. Volunteer housing may be available during certain periods of the year. Job descriptions are varied. The park attempts to match the interest of individuals with the needs of the park. Biological Assistants (Bird Inventories, Insect Inventories, etc.), Exotic Plant Technicians (Inventory, Map, and Control exotic plants), Visitor Center Information Desk Volunteers, Natural History Interpreters and Living History Interpreters are among the staff regularly recruited.

Sewee Visitor and Environmental Education Center

Agency: U.S. Fish and Wildlife Service
Season: Year-round
Contact: Janna Larson
5821 Hwy. 17 N.
Awendaw, SC 29429
E-mail: jannalarson@fs.fed.us
Web: seweecenter.fws.gov
Phone: (843) 928–3368

Description/Positions Available: We are located approximately 20 miles north of the historic city of Charleston on Highway 17 North in Awendaw. The Sewee Visitor Center is a partnership between the U.S. Fish and Wildlife Service, Cape Romain National Wildlife Refuge and the USDA Forest Service and Francis Marion National Forest. The two agencies oversee approximately 315,000 acres of upland pine forest to salt marsh and barrier island habitat.

Volunteers are needed for Interpretation, Resource Management, Visitor Services, and Maintenance.

South Dakota

Bureau of Land Management, Belle Fourche Office

Agency: Bureau of Land Management
Contact: Nancy Rime
310 Roundup St.
Belle Fourche, SD 57717
E-mail: nrime@mt.blm.gov
Phone: (605) 892–7000

Description/Positions Available: The Bureau of Land Management office is located in Belle Fourche on Highway 85 North of I–95.

Please contact us for current volunteer opportunities.

Custer State Park

Agency: State parks
Season: Mostly mid-May to Labor Day or beyond. Some winter opportunities.
Contact: Craig Pugsley
HC 83, P.O. Box 70
Custer, SD 57730
E-mail: Craig.Pugsley@state.sd.us
Web: www.state.sd.us/sdparks
Phone: (605) 255–4515

Description/Positions Available: This 73,000-acre park features an outstanding cross-section of Black Hills topography and supports stands of ponderosa pine, spruce, and hardwoods. Abundant wildlife includes deer, elk, bighorn sheep, pronghorn antelope, mountain goats, and one of the nation's largest buffalo herds.

We need volunteers to serve as Visitor Center Hosts, Office Assistants, Trails Assistants, Information Hosts, Maintenance Assistants and Campground Hosts. Benefits include housing (free campsite with full hookups for 24 hours/week), training, uniform, supervision, and equipment. Housing for college-age individuals may be available at no cost.

Mount Rushmore National Memorial

Agency: National Park Service
Season: Year-round
Contact: Bruce Mellberg
P.O. Box 268
Keystone, SD 57751-0268
E-mail: bruce_mellberg@nps.gov
Web: www.nps.gov/moru/index.htm
Phone: (605) 574–3151

Description/Positions Available: Mount Rushmore National Memorial preserves and protects Gutzon Borglum's sculptural masterpiece, commemorating the first 150 years of our nation's history with the mountain carving of four presidents.

We are looking for an Interpretive Volunteer or Student Intern to research, develop, and present interpretive talks, walks, and school programs. The responsibilities of this post will also include staffing the information desk at the museum and information center. Housing is provided as is a subsistence stipend. We also need a Museum Intern to perform cataloging, environmental monitoring duties, and to work directly with the collection on a series of assigned projects. This position's duration is 12–24 weeks, 40 hours per week. For more specific details on these positions please visit our Web site or give us a call.

South Dakota State Parks

Agency: State parks
Season: Spring through fall
Contact: Lynn Spomer
523 E. Capitol Ave.
Pierre, SD 57501
E-mail: lynn.spomer@state.sd.us
Web: www.state.sd.us/sdparks
Phone: (605) 773–3391

Description/Positions Available: More than 100 volunteer opportunities exist in forty state parks across the state of South Dakota. These positions will allow for free camping if you agree to work a minimum of twenty-four hours per week per person for thirty days. Many different opportunities are also available for internships. You must be at college sophomore standing or have completed one year of vocational school.

Campground Hosts, Maintenance Workers, Office Assistants, Special Project Volunteers, Program Volunteers and Visitor Center Volunteers are all needed.

U.S. Army Corps of Engineers, Gavins Point Project

Agency: USCOA
Season: Summer
Contact: David L. Mines, Park Ranger
P.O. Box 710
Yankton, SD 57078
E-mail: david.l.mines@usace.army.mil or gavinspoint@usace.army.mil
Web: www.nwo.usace.army.mil/html/Lake_Proj/gavinspoint/welcome.html

Description/Positions Available: We operate in the vicinity of the last of six dams on the Missouri River. This area features a lake surrounded by wooded chalkstone bluffs explored by Lewis and Clark on their journey westward. Campground Hosts are needed in developed campground areas 4 miles west of Yankton. Applicants will assist visitors, dispense information, assist with interpretive programs, and perform minor maintenance duties. Volunteers must enjoy meeting people and walking long distances. You must provide your own camper. Benefits include access to a free campsite with electrical hookups only, and a chance to meet and visit with some wonderful people. Positions are available from Memorial Day to Labor Day. One month is the maximum duration of all positions.

Wind Cave National Park

Agency: National Park Service
Season: Summer
Contact: Phyllis Cremonini, Volunteer Coordinator
RR 1, Box 190
Hot Springs, SD 57747
E-mail: phyllis_cremonini@nps.gov
Web: www.nps.gov/wica/
Phone: (605) 745–4600

Description/Positions Available: Located in the southern Black Hills, this park features some of the most pristine mixed grass prairie found in the United States. Large herds of fee-roaming bison, elk, pronghorn, and deer inhabit the grasslands and forest. Wind Cave contains beautiful formations, including rare boxwork, cave popcorn, dogtooth spar, and frostwork. It is currently the sixth-largest cave network in the world.

Internships are available for Park Ranger-Interpretation positions. Associated duties include a full range of interpretive programs and activities. Interns will be responsible for researching, developing, and presenting four different thematic cave tours; staffing the visitor center information desk; developing and presenting interpretive programs and prairie hikes; offering information and orientation services in informal settings such as parking lots and outdoor terraces; and assisting with special projects. Interns will receive rent-free housing, a uniform allowance, participation in interpretive training, up to $150 for round-trip travel to the park, and a stipend of $75 per week for the thirteen-week assignment. College credit may be available by making arrangements with your college advisor following selection for the program. The internships begin May 20 and end August 17, 2002. The application deadline is March 1, 2002.

Wind Cave National Park

Agency: National Park Service
Season: Year-round
Contact: Phyllis Cremonini, Volunteer Coordinator
RR 1, Box 190
Hot Springs, SD 57747
E-mail: phyllis_cremonini@nps.gov
Web: www.nps.gov/wica/
Phone: (605) 745–4600

Description/Positions Available: Located in the southern Black Hills, this park features some of the most pristine mixed grass prairie found in the United States. Large herds of free-roaming bison, elk, pronghorn, and deer inhabit the grasslands and forest. Wind Cave contains beautiful formations, including rare boxwork, cave popcorn, dogtooth spar and frostwork. It is currently the sixth largest cave network in the world.

We recruit for year-round positions in Interpretation/Visitor Services. Duties include conducting cave tours, staffing the information desk, and presenting interpretive programs. Summer opportunities also include openings for Campground Hosts. Hosts provide information and visitor services at the seventy-five site campgrounds. Limited positions are also available in Resource Management with duties such as wildlife observation and monitoring, cave inventory, exploration and surveying, and vegetation inventories. Benefits include training, park housing or campsite provision, and a small stipend.

Tennessee

Big South Fork National River and Recreation Area

Agency: National Park Service
Season: Summer
Contact: Susan Duncan
4564 Leatherwood Rd.
Oneida, TN 37841
E-mail: sue_duncan@nps.gov
Web: www.nps.gov/biso
Phone: (931) 879–4890

Description/Positions Available: Bandy Creek Campground.

We need Campground Hosts. Your duties require that you be available a minimum of four weeks with twenty-four hours committed per week. You will assist visitors with registration, area specific and general information and will serve as a

contact for emergencies. A site will be provided for you with water and sewer facilities. Positions are available from April until October.

Cherokee National Forest, Nolichucky, Unaka District

Agency: U.S. Department of Agriculture Forest Service
Season: Summer
Contact: Cheryl Summers
4900 Ashville Hwy. SR 70
Greeneville, TN 37743
Web: www.southernregion.fs.fed.us/cherokee/default.htm
Phone: (423) 638–4109

Description/Positions Available: Located in Carter, Washington, Unicoi, Greene and Cocke counties in the mountains of eastern Tennessee, this recreation area features premium fishing in a number of cold-water trout streams and in nearby warm-water rivers and lakes. Trails and other points of interest are nearby.

Campground Hosts are needed for Horse Creek, Paint Creek, Rock Creek, and Round Mountain recreation areas for the summer camping season. Duties include greeting visitors, providing information, explaining regulations, and performing minor maintenance. Participation in interpretive programs is optional. Applicants must be at least eighteen years old and have their own camper or trailer. The Horse Creek Recreation host site and Rock Creek have electricity, water, telephone, and gray-water wells.

Cherokee National Forest, Ocoee District

Agency: U.S. Department of Agriculture Forest Service
Season: Summer
Contact: Steve Goldman
Rt.1, Box 348D
Benton, TN 37307
Web: www.southernregion.fs.fed.us/cherokee/default.htm
Phone: (423) 338–5201

Description/Positions Available: Campground Hosts are needed. Please contact the district for more details.

Cherokee National Forest, Tellico District

Agency: U.S. Department of Agriculture Forest Service
Season: Summer
Contact: Volunteer Coordinator
250 Ranger Station Rd.
Tellico Plains, TN 37385
Web: www.southernregion.fs.fed.us/cherokee/default.htm

Phone: (423) 253–2520

Description/Positions Available: Campground Hosts are needed. Please contact the district for more details.

Cherokee National Forest, Watuga District

Agency: U.S. Department of Agriculture Forest Service
Season: Summer
Contact: Amy Fore
P.O. Box 400
Unicoi, TN 37692
Web: www.southernregion.fs.fed.us/cherokee/default.htm
Phone: (423) 735–1500

Description/Positions Available: Covering 140,000 acres in northeastern Tennessee, this district includes two large lakes, two wilderness areas, 150 miles of trail (including 50 miles of the Appalachian Trail), four campgrounds, five picnic areas and three swimming areas. Elevations range from 1,700 to 4,900 feet. Topography includes mountain peaks and slopes, sheltered coves, and cold-water streams and ponds.

Campground Hosts are needed for Little Oak and Jacobs Creek campgrounds at South Holston Lake, Carden's Bluff Campground at Watauga Lake and Backbone Rock in Johnson County. Duties may include gate management, visitor information and light maintenance. Two to six long-term hosts needed from April or May to late fall. Amenities may include waived fees and electricity at site.

Nashville District, U.S. Army Corps of Engineers

Agency: USCOA
Season: Year-round
Contact: Volunteer Clearinghouse
P.O. Box 1070
Nashville, TN 37202

E-mail: Gayla.Mitchell@lrn02.usace.army.mil
Web: www.orn.usace.army.mil/volunteer
Phone: (800) 865–8337

Description/Positions Available: The Nashville District features ten beautiful lakes in Kentucky and Tennessee with numerous parks and campgrounds.

We are offering volunteer opportunities for Campground or Park Hosts, Visitor Center Staff, Park or Trail Maintenance Workers, Shoreline Cleanup Workers, Office Assistants, and Fish and Wildlife Restoration Workers. A free campsite is often provided!

Reelfoot National Wildlife Refuge

Agency: U.S. Fish and Wildlife Service
Season: Year-round
Contact: Christine Donald
4343 Hwy. 157
Union City, TN 38261
E-mail: Christine_Donald@fws.gov
Web: reelfoot.fws.gov
Phone: (731) 538–2481

Description/Positions Available: Reelfoot NWR in Union City, Tennessee is looking for volunteers. If you have an RV, fifth wheel, or travel there are full-hookups sites available in exchange for labor. Laundry facilities and use of

a government vehicle for work purposes will also be provided.

Indoor and outdoor work is available. Indoor: Assist in the visitor center greeting visitors, stocking brochures, answering the phone, light typing, etc. Outdoor: Assist in landscaping (mowing, pruning, weeding) and in trail maintenance, nest box making, painting, etc.

Stones River National Battlefield

Agency: National Park Service
Season: Year-round
Contact: Volunteer Coordinator
3501 Old Nashville Hwy.
Murfreesboro, TN 37129
E-mail: stri_information@nps.gov
Web: www.nps.gov/stri
Phone: (615) 893–9501

Description/Positions Available: Stones River National Battlefield is located in the center of the state in Murfreesboro, Tennessee. It is the site of a bloody mid-winter Civil War battle between the Army of the Cumberland Union (General William S. Rosecrans) and Confederate Army of Tennessee (General Braxton Bragg.)

Museum Technicians, Biological Technicians, Resource Management Workers, Maintenance Workers, and Interpreters are all needed.

Texas

Amistad National Recreation Area

Agency: National Park Service
Season: Year-round
Contact: Erik Finkelstein
HCR 3 Box 5J
Del Rio, TX 78840
E-mail: amis_interpretation@nps.gov
Web: www.nps.gov/amis

Phone: (830) 775–7491

Description/Positions Available: This 58,000-acre water-based park is located in southwestern Texas along the Mexican border. Mild winters and excellent boating, fishing, swimming, picnicking, waterskiing, birding, and camping make the winter months this area's busiest.

Campground Hosts are needed between December and April to dispense information, patrol the campgrounds, and explain rules and regulations. Applicants must provide their own trailer/RV and commit to thirty-two hours per week in exchange for reimbursement for propane or gas. Radios are provided. Volunteers also needed for maintenance projects year-round and visitor center duties. Interpretation Volunteers are also needed between October and March. RV sites are available for holders of this position.

Chamizal National Memorial

Agency: National Park Service
Season: Year-round
Contact: Fannie Baca
800 S. San Marcial
El Paso, TX 79905
E-mail: Fannie_Baca@nps.gov
Web: www.nps.gov/cham
Phone: (915) 532–7273

Description/Positions Available: Chamizal National Memorial is an urban park located in south central El Paso, just north of the Rio Grande and immediately adjacent to the international boundary. The visitor center is located in the center of the grounds. Employees of the National Park Service are on hand to answer questions. The visitor center complex also includes a bookstore, a 500-seat theater, the Los Paisanos Gallery, and a courtyard with a garden and fountain. A lighted parking area is provided on the grounds. Picnicking is permitted, but there are no overnight camping facilities. The visitor center is open from 8:00 A.M. to 5:00 P.M. There is no fee for admission to the park. Throughout the year the National Park Service sponsors special programs and activities to broaden understanding and to encourage perpetuation of cultural heritages in the performing and graphic arts. Professionals and outstanding amateurs of both countries present theater performances in the fields of ballet, folk, drama, music, and other arts.

To make all this possible, we are in need of Administrative, Clerical, and Interpretive personnel.

Fort Davis National Historic Site

Agency: National Park Service
Season: Year-round
Contact: Superintendent
P.O. Box 1456
Fort Davis, TX 79734
E-mail: foda_ranger_activities@nps.gov
Phone: (915) 426–3224

Description/Positions Available: Regarded as the most outstanding surviving example of a southwestern frontier military post, Fort Davis protected travelers and the mail from attacks on the San Antonio/El Paso Road from 1854 to 1891.

Volunteers are needed year-round for Interpretation (including doing living history, working with school groups on and off-site, staffing visitor center desk and developing media presentations), Library and Museum work, Maintenance (including carpentry), Administration (including computer entry and microfilm indexing), and Historic Trail Maintenance. Living History Interpreters are needed in March and during summer (Memorial Day to Labor Day) to interpret and keep open restored and refurbished buildings, conduct demonstrations in period clothing, and participate in special events. Benefits include the provision of a trailer site with electricity and sewage hookups as available, with preference given to those volunteering a minimum of thirty-two hours per week.

Guadalupe Mountains National Park

Agency: National Park Service
Season: Year-round
Contact: VIP Coordinator
HC 60, Box 400
Salt Flat, TX 79847
Phone: (915) 828–3251, extension 105

Description/Positions Available: The Guadalupe Mountains formed as a type of barrier reef during the Permian Period some 250 million years ago. Today, standing like an island in the desert, the mountains and canyons shelter a unique variety of plants and animals. This area offers a backdrop for the study of life sciences and geological history.

Campground Hosts are needed year-round at Pine Springs and Dog Canyon campgrounds. Applicants should note that an RV is required. Park Maintenance Aides are needed for ongoing repair and maintenance. Visitor Center Assistants are also needed year-round for visitor-center operations and other interesting jobs. Administration Aides are needed for general office duties such as light typing, word processing, and filing. All safety and work equipment is provided. Benefits include free housing if available, training, supervision, and worker's insurance.

National Park Service/Amtrak

Agency: National Park Service
Season: Year-round
Contact: Lisa Evans
HCR 3, Box 5J
Del Rio, TX 78840-9350
E-mail: Mike_Casler@nps.gov
Phone: (830) 775–7491, extension 223

Description/Positions Available: See description under Nationwide listings in the front of this directory.

This program is presented on board Amtrak's "Sunset Limited" between Del Rio and Alpine, Texas. We need Trails & Rails volunteers to ride once a month between these two cities. There are no housing, camping or lodging facilities provided by the program. The only expenses covered are those associated with the actual program.

Utah

Bryce Canyon National Park

Agency: National Park Service
Season: Year-round
Contact: James Woolsey
P.O. Box 17001
Bryce Canyon, UT 84717
E-mail: James_Woolsey@nps.gov
Web: www.nps.gov/brca
Phone: (434) 435–4410

Description/Positions Available: Bryce Canyon National Park, located in southern Utah, has ideal summers, with cool fall and winter temperatures and winters bringing lots of snow. The park preserves the amazing geology associated with the eroding plateau where the park is located. For more details on the park please visit our Web site.

Bryce typically has more than 100 volunteers per year doing many tasks including visitor center services, backcountry and front-country patrols, maintenance, administration, librarianship, and others. Please contact our volunteer coordinator for specific information on available opportunities.

Bureau of Land Management, Price Field Office

Agency: Bureau of Land Management
Season: Year-round
Contact: Dennis Willis
125 South 600 W.
Price, UT 84501
E-mail: Dennis_Willis@blm.gov
Web: www.ut.blm.gov/volunteerannc.html

Description/Positions Available: The Price Field Office is located in southeastern Utah. Features include the San Rafael Swell, Desolation Canyon, the Book Cliffs, Nine Mile Canyon, and Cleveland-Lloyd Dinosaur Quarry. We are recruiting River Rangers for Desolation Canyon. We also need volunteers for backcountry patrols in the San Rafael Swell. Visitor

Contact personnel are needed year-round for Cleveland-Lloyd Dinosaur Quarry.

Bureau of Land Management, Price Field Office

Agency: Bureau of Land Management
Season: Spring through summer
Contact: Ann Lambertsen
125 South 600 W.
Price, UT 84501
E-mail: Ann_Lambertsen@blm.gov
Web: www.ut.blm.gov/volunteerannc.html
Phone: (435) 636-3633

Description/Positions Available: The Cleveland-Lloyd Dinosaur Quarry is one of the world's most significant discoveries of Jurassic dinosaurs. More than 12,000 bones representing at least sixty-eight individual animals and eleven species have been recovered from this active, working quarry. In addition to the quarry, there is a visitor center, picnic area and interpretive hiking trail. Approximately 5,000 visitors per year tour the quarry and visitor center.

We offer intern/volunteer opportunity in Recreation/Paleontology. Two volunteers are needed between Easter and Labor Day or a portion thereof. These people would assist in the operation of the Cleveland-Lloyd Dinosaur Quarry. This opportunity would be ideal for students who need to fulfill an internship. Friends or couples are welcome to apply. A five-month commitment starting at Easter would be preferred, but eight-week time frames are acceptable. For more information visit our Web site or give us a call.

Bureau of Land Management, Salt Lake Field Office

Agency: Bureau of Land Management
Season: Year-round
Contact: Tina King
2370 S. 2300 W.
Salt Lake City, UT 84119
E-mail: t1king@ut.blm.gov

Web: www.ut.blm.gov/volunteerannc.html

Description/Positions Available: The Bureau of Land Management's Salt Lake Field Office manages 3,240,221 acres of Great Basin Landscape, including Bureau of Land Management land located in the counties of Box Elder, Cache, Rich, Weber, Davis, Morgan, Tooele, Salt Lake, Summit, Wasatch, and Utah in Northern Utah. The agency's management responsibilities include recreation, commercial activities, natural and cultural heritage resources, historical sites, fish and wildlife habitat, wild horse and burro populations, wilderness areas, restoring at risk resources and reducing threats to public health, safety, and property.

There are currently Receptionist, Clerical and Administrative Support opportunities available. For more information please visit our Web site or give us a call.

Bureau of Land Management, St. George Field Office

Agency: Bureau of Land Management
Season: Summer
Contact: R. J. Hughes
345 East Riverside Dr.
St George, UT 84790
E-mail: RJ_Hughes@blm.gov
Web: www.ut.blm.gov/volunteerannc.html
Phone: (435) 688-3210

Description/Positions Available: A Campground Host is needed at the Red Cliffs campground north of St. George, Utah.

Two volunteers are needed between Easter and Labor Day or a portion thereof. These people would assist in the operation of the Cleveland-Lloyd Dinosaur Quarry. This opportunity would be ideal for students who need to fulfill an internship. Friends or couples are welcome to apply. A five-month commitment starting at Easter would be preferred, but eight-week time frames are acceptable.

Bureau of Land Management, Vernal Field Office

Agency: Bureau of Land Management
Season: Summer
Contact: Dave Moore
170 S. 500 E.
Vernal, UT 84078
E-mail: Dave_Moore@blm.gov
Web: www.ut.blm.gov/volunteerannc.html
Phone: (435) 781-4473

Description/Positions Available: The Bureau of Land Management Vernal Field Office is currently recruiting volunteers for the Browns Park at the John Jarvie Historic Site and Green River Recreation Complex.

There are Recreation/Paleontology opportunities available.

Manti–La Sal National Forest

Agency: U.S. Department of Agriculture Forest Service
Season: Summer
Contact: Ken Straley
599 W. Price River Dr.
Price, UT 84501
E-mail: kstraley@fs.fed.us
Web: www.fs.fed.us/r4/mantilasal/
Phone: (435) 636-3541

Description/Positions Available: Located in south central and southern Utah, the Manti–La Sal National Forest includes the high, rolling hills of the Wasatch Plateau, the dramatic La Sal Mountains near the recreation Mecca of Moab, and the ponderosa forests of the Abajo Mountains high above the canyon country of Cedar Mesa and Canyonlands. Elevations range from about 6,000 feet to more than 12,000 feet, creating an extremely diverse and rugged landscape and offering varied and almost limitless recreational opportunities.

Trail Hound wanted! We need one volunteer to assist in a forest-wide trail inventory and condition survey from May to September of 2002. Duty

hours may be five days per week or eight-day tours. Most of the work can be completed on a daily basis, returning home each night, but some will require overnight backpacking or car camping for up to three days. Extensive hiking (often carrying weight) will be required. The duty station for this position will vary across the Manti–La Sal National Forest throughout the summer. The volunteer will receive $16 per diem and lodging, if needed. A self-contained travel trailer or motor home is preferable but not necessary.

Timpanogos Cave National Monument

Agency: National Park Service
Season: Year-round
Contact: Chief Ranger
RR 3, Box 200
American Fork, UT 84003
Phone: (801) 756-5239

Description/Positions Available: This park features three small caves connected by man-made tunnels located high on the canyon wall of American Fork Canyon. Delicate and colorful cave formations delight visitors who make the strenuous hike to the caves. This 250-acre, day-use-only monument is a short forty-minute drive from Salt Lake City (thirty minutes from Provo) and receives fewer than 140,000 visitors annually.

We have opportunities for Cave Tour Interpretation, Resource Management, Maintenance, Visitor Information Services and Administrative Support currently available. Benefits include training, job experience, working in a beautiful setting, and mileage reimbursement. Housing is not available in the monument but may be available in nearby communities.

Uinta National Forest, Heber Ranger District

Agency: U.S. Department of Agriculture Forest Service
Season: Spring to fall

Contact: Patricia Musser
P.O. Box 190
Heber City, UT 84032
Phone: (435) 654–0470

Description/Positions Available: This district is located east of Heber City and offers beautiful scenery, hiking trails including part of the Great Western Trail, well-maintained campgrounds near reservoirs, great fishing opportunities, and plenty of wildlife.

Volunteers are needed for Trail Maintenance and Trail Construction, Wildlife Survey, Range and Timber.

USDA Forest Service

Agency: U.S. Department of Agriculture Forest Service
Season: Year-round
Contact: Gene Watson
324 25th St.
Ogden, UT 84401
E-mail: gwatson@fs.fed.us
Web: www.fs.fed.us/r4/volunteer/positions.html
Phone: (801) 625–5175

Description/Positions Available: The Intermountain Region of the Forest Service has many volunteer opportunities in the national forests located within the states of Idaho, Nevada, Utah, and Wyoming. The Rocky Mountain Research Station also has quite a few needs for volunteers in these states as does the state of Montana. These volunteer needs are individually listed in our volunteer directory for the sixteen national forests and eight Forestry Science Labs in those states.

Some of the forty categories of volunteer requests include: Archeology (Passport in Time), Backcountry Ranger, Campground Host and Maintenance, Facilities Maintenance, Fire Management and Prevention, Guard Station Attendant, Hydrology/Watershed, Information/Education, Landscape Architecture, Maintenance Work, Minerals Management, Office Work, Public Affairs Assistant, Range Management, Recreation Aid, Resource Assistant, Soil Scientist Timber Management, Trail Maintenance/Construction, Visitor Center Attendant, Volunteer Coordinator, Wilderness Information Specialist, Wildlife and Fish Management, Winter Sports Assistant. The volunteer directory lists the location of the opportunity, the address and telephone number of the person to contact, and provides information concerning the work, any living accommodations that might be available, and any subsistence offered to help cover expenses. When requesting a copy of the volunteer directory, mention that you read about it in AHS's "Helping Out in the Outdoors", and we will send you a free map of the Intermountain Region with your Volunteer Directory.

Wasatch-Cache Nation Forest, Kamas Ranger District

Agency: U.S. Department of Agriculture Forest Service
Season: Summer
Contact: Barbara Walker
P.O. Box 68
Kamas, UT 84036
E-mail: bwalker02@fs.fed.us
Web: www.fs.fed.us/wcnf/
Phone: (435) 783–4338

Description/Positions Available: Kamas Ranger District is located in northern Utah on the western end of the Uinta Mountains. Kamas is approximately 45 miles east of Salt Lake City and 15 miles east of Park City. The Uintas are Utah's highest mountains with peak altitudes between 11,000 and 13,000 feet. High alpine meadows and glaciated lakes are scattered throughout the upper elevations.

Two to four positions for Wilderness/backcountry Rangers are currently being offered to make zero-impact educational contacts with visitors and do light trail work. Rangers camp in tents for three to four nights per week between June and August. We are also looking to fill two to four positions on a trail crew. This job involves building boardwalks and doing rock work between June and August 1. Finally, we offer a position for one individual to work with Boy Scouts on service projects, particularly Eagle projects during a similar time frame.

Vermont

Green Mountain Club

Agency: NON PRO
Season: Year-round
Contact: Director of Field Programs
4711 Waterbury-Stowe Rd.
Waterbury Center, VT 05677
E-mail: dave@greenmountainclub.org
Web: www.greenmountainclub.org
Phone: (802) 244–7037

Description/Positions Available: The Green Mountain Club maintains hundreds of miles of hiking trails throughout Vermont including the Long Trail (the original long-distance backpacking trail) and a portion of the Appalachian Trail. This trail system includes seventy-nine backcountry cabins and primitive campsites, which the GMC manages all aspects of (for example, we are leaders in the field of composting outhouses). Our trails thread through the famous Vermont landscape of green pastures, small villages, expansive northern forest, and rocky-topped mountains. Though the mountains seem gentle from a distance, trails here are steep and rugged. Two-hundred-thousand people a year camp and hike in the Green Mountains, and the GMC educates them in low-impact skills that keep the trails wild for the future.

The Green Mountain Club has dozens of full-time seasonal positions living and working outside in the Vermont Mountains. Caretakers do the demanding work of protecting beautiful, fragile places, caring for campsites, and educating hikers about them. The Long Trail Patrol trail crew forms a tight-knit group that does the heavy work of building trails using hand tools and primitive skills. Folks can commit to work for as short as one week or as long as four months. Most work is during the period May through October. Housing, food, and/or a stipend are provided.

Green Mountain National Forest

Agency: U.S. Department of Agriculture Forest Service
Season: Summer
Contact: Kathleen Diehl
231 North Main St.
Rutland, VT 05701
E-mail: kdiehl@fs.fed.us
Web: www.fs.fed.us/r9/gmfl/
Phone: (802) 747–6709

Description/Positions Available: The forest's scenic beauty along the backbone of Vermont's Green Mountains offers unlimited recreation opportunities during any season of the year. Whether you are a hiker, skier, camper, fishing or hunting enthusiast, or wildlife watcher, the Green Mountain National Forest can provide the recreational experience you are seeking!

Frontliners help in our visitor information centers to greet people, answer phone calls, and distribute information to potential visitors. We also need six Campground Hosts. An Environmental Assessment volunteer is also needed to work with Forest Planning on the new revision of the Forest Management Plan. Volunteer should have at least basic knowledge about environmental assessments. We always need Trail Maintenance volunteers.

National Park Service/Amtrak

Agency: National Park Service
Season: Summer

Contact: Trails & Rails Coordinator
One Armory Square
Springfield, MA 01105-1299
E-mail: Superintendent_SPAR@nps.gov
Phone: (413) 734–6477

Description/Positions Available: See description under Nationwide listings in the front of this directory.

This program is presented on board Amtrak's "Vermonter" between St. Albans, Vermont and Springfield, Massachusetts. We need Trails & Rails volunteers to ride once a month between these two cities. There are no housing, camping or lodging facilities provided by the program. The only expenses covered are those associated with the actual program.

Virginia

Appalachian Trail Conference

Agency: NON PRO
Season: Year-round
Contact: Jody L. Bickel
P.O. Box 10
Newport, VA 24128
E-mail: crews@appalachiantrail.org
Web: www.appalachiantrail.org
Phone: (540) 544–7388

Description/Positions Available: Help build a piece of the Appalachian National Scenic Trail (AT). Winding along the peaks of the Appalachians from Georgia to Maine, the AT exists thanks to countless dedicated volunteers who planned, constructed and now maintain and manage the trail and surrounding lands through the Appalachian Trail Conference, a non-profit organization.

Participate in the AT project by joining one of ATC's five Volunteer Trail Crews, operated in

Vermont State Parks

Agency: State parks
Season: Summer
Contact: Craig Whipple, Chief of Park Operations
103 S. Main St.–10 South
Waterbury, VT 05671
E-mail: cwhipple@fpr.anr.state.vt.us
Web: www.vtstateparks.com
Phone: (802) 241–3655

Description/Positions Available: Fifty-two parks are located throughout Vermont, near lakes, ponds, rivers and streams, in wooded settings, and on islands.

We are recruiting for Park Attendant positions. These jobs involve helping to clean restrooms and campsites, mowing lawns, improving trails, greeting visitors, and doing nature programs, etc.

cooperation with the United States Forest Service, the National Park Service and AT Maintaining Clubs. A professional crew leader directs the crews in designing and building new trail segments, rehabilitating damaged treadway, constructing quality rockwork, and building friendships that can last a lifetime. Volunteer for a week or a whole season. No experience is necessary. ATC provides the training, room and board. Crews operate between May and October, from base camps in Great Smoky Mountains National Park, Southwestern Virginia, Central Pennsylvania, Vermont, and Northern Maine. You must be eighteen years or older.

Appalachian Trail Conference

Agency: NON PRO
Season: Year-round
Contact: Trail Crew Program
P.O. Box 10
Newport, VA 24128

E-mail: crews@appalachiantrail.org
Web: www.appalachiantrail.org
Phone: (540) 544–7388

Description/Positions Available: Join us in stewardship of the famous Appalachian Trail, a National Scenic Trail and a unit of the National Park System. The Appalachian Trail Conference operates five seasonal Volunteer Trail Crews along the length of the trail. The crews are based in northern Maine, central Vermont, Pennsylvania, southwestern Virginia, and the Great Smoky Mountains of Tennessee. Week-long crews work on projects such as trail relocations, erosion control, treadway rehabilitation, bridge and shelter construction, and rockwork. After arriving at the base camp, volunteers are provided with food, camping equipment, transportation, tools, and safety gear. Crews are supervised by professional crew leaders, skilled in trail construction, chainsaw use, first aid, and outdoor leadership. The crews work in partnership with local ATC affiliated trail clubs that maintain particular sections of the footpath. Participate in the crew program and gain trail construction skills, outdoor experience, and lots of lasting, fun-filled memories. No experience is required, just a willingness to work hard and learn new skills, and a community-minded spirit. Applicants must be eighteen years or older. See our Web site, e-mail, call our office for a crew program application or to gain more information about crew leader and assistant crew leader positions.

Positions available include Crew Leaders, Assistant Crew Leaders, and Camp Coordinators. For more information on these seasonal positions see our Web site for a 2002 application or contact our office for more details. These positions are guaranteed to provide a quality, fun-filled experience to all. Join us on our staff for a great 2002 Volunteer Trail Crew season.

Booker T. Washington National Monument

Agency: National Park Service
Season: Year-round
Contact: Betsy Haynes
12130 Booker T. Washington Hwy.
Hardy, VA 24101
E-mail: alice_hanawalt@nps.gov
Web: www.nps.gov/bowa

Description/Positions Available: We are located in Franklin County, near the Blue Ridge Parkway and Smith Mountain Lake, 25 miles southeast of Roanoke.

Farm Aides are needed to assists with historic farming operations. A costumed Interpreter is also required to assist with living history programs. Finally, we are looking for a Visitor Services Aide to assist in the running of the visitor center.

Bureau of Land Management

Agency: Bureau of Land Management
Season: Fall
Contact: Joe Zilincar
Bureau of Land Management-ES,
7450 Boston Blvd.
Springfield, VA 22153
E-mail: Joe_Zilincar@es.blm.gov
Web: www.blm.gov/nhp/index.htm
Phone: (703) 440–1717

Description/Positions Available: We need volunteers on National Public Lands Day at a variety of sites in northern Virginia. This takes place on the last Saturday of September each year.

Volunteer duties will include the rehabilitation of hiking trails, implementing strategies to control erosion, replanting and reseeding high use areas, and other outdoor tasks on public lands.

Chincoteague National Wildlife Refuge

Agency: U.S. Fish and Wildlife Service
Season: Year-round

Contact: Geralyn Mireles
P.O. Box 62
Chincoteague, VA 23336
E-mail: Geralyn_Mireles@fws.gov
Web: www.chinco.fws.gov
Phone: (757) 336–6122

Description/Positions Available: Chincoteague National Wildlife Refuge is offering internships. Have you ever dreamed about working on an island? Do you enjoy the beach and the outdoors? Do you want to be involved in educating people about the National Wildlife Refuge System—the largest system of lands set aside specifically for wildlife? Are you interested in protecting our natural resources? If you have answered yes to any of these questions, have we got opportunities for you! Chincoteague National Wildlife Refuge includes more than 14,000 acres of beach, dunes, marsh, and maritime forest. Most of the refuge is located on the Virginia end of Assateague Island. Chincoteague Refuge is one of the most visited refuges in the United States, providing visitors with outstanding opportunities to learn about and enjoy wildlands and wildlife. Refuge management programs restore threatened and endangered species, such as the piping plover, and conserve local wildlife and plants. The refuge also provides environmental education and wildlife-dependent recreational opportunities such as fishing, hunting, wildlife observation, interpretation, and wildlife photography.

Interpretive Internships are available in spring, summer, and fall. You will staff the Refuge Visitor Center and develop and conduct interpretive programs as well as other informational material. These duties provide interns with the opportunity to reach diverse groups of people with a knowledge and appreciation of the environment and the National Wildlife Refuge System. Applicants should have a background in biology, wildlife management, recreation education, interpretation, or a related field. Applicants must have experience speaking in front of groups, knowledge of animal and plant identification (especially birds), and have the ability to communicate well in writing. The application deadline for spring (mid March to mid-June) is January 15. The deadline for summer (late May to early September) and for fall (late August to early December) is March 15. Environmental Education Internships are also available. Interns work directly with the refuge's education staff. You will prepare and present curriculum-based environmental education (EE) programs for school and youth groups, develop teaching aids, and assist with teacher workshops. Applicants should have a background in biology, wildlife management, education, recreation, or a related field and experience working with young people in an outdoor setting. Good oral and written communication skills are required. Applicants must be comfortable speaking in front of groups. Application deadlines for Spring (mid-March to early June) fall on January 1. Field Research Assistant/Wildlife Management Internships: The refuge offers field research assistant internships will be taking place during the summer and fall. Interns are involved in an array of biological activities including collecting data and monitoring a population of the threatened piping plover. Duties include the following: weekly population surveys; nest searches; behavioral observations; nest monitoring; ghost crab and predator monitoring; vegetation transects; waterfowl surveys; and data collection at deer check station. There will be instances where the intern will have the opportunity to participate in other ongoing refuge management programs and studies. Applicants should be recent graduates or students (Junior status) in wildlife biology, ecology, environmental biology, general biology, natural resource management, or related field. Communication skills, writing skills, a desire to work with people, good observational and recording skills, and a valid driver's license are all required. Experience working with shorebirds, waterfowl and wading birds, or a background in ornithology and general biology and a knowledge of computers are all desirable. The application deadline for this summer (mid-May to mid-August) is March 15. The fall (early September to late November) deadline is August 1. Dates are flexible, but you must begin no later than June 1 for summer interns and October 1 for fall interns. All internships pay $100 per week, and housing is provided. Internships are a twelve-week commitment; however, the refuge can be flexible when deemed necessary. To apply, send a resume and cover letter to Chincoteague National Wildlife Refuge Attention: Volunteer Coordinator P.O. Box 62 Chincoteague, VA 23336. Please specify which internship you are interested in. Other opportunities not listed above may be available throughout the year. Contact the refuge Volunteer Coordinator at (757) 336–6122 for more information.

Eastern Shore of Virginia National Wildlife Refuge

Agency: U.S. Fish and Wildlife Service
Season: Year-round
Contact: Jim Kenyon
5003 Hallett Circle
Cape Charles, VA 23310
Phone: (757) 331–2760

Description/Positions Available: The refuge is located on the southern tip of the Delmarva Peninsula, bordering both the Chesapeake Bay and Atlantic Ocean.

Environmental Education/Wildlife Biologist Interns are needed for twelve weeks to staff a visitor center information desk (30 percent); conduct wildlife surveys and record data (25 percent); develop and conduct environmental-education programs (20 percent); design wildlife exhibits and flyers (10 percent); maintain trails and manage habitats (10 percent); and maintain saltwater and freshwater aquariums in the environmental-education labs (5 percent). A strong background in wildlife biology or any natural-resource area, some experience working with the public, and good people skills are preferred qualifications. You will be paid a total of $1200. Housing is provided on refuge lands. Personal transportation is required as a condition of employment. Send your resume with three references.

Fredericksburg and Spotsylvania National Military Park

Agency: National Park Service
Season: Year-round
Contact: Greg Mertz, Supervisory Historian
120 Chatham Lane
Fredericksburg, VA 22405
E-mail: greg_mertz@nps.gov
Web: www.nps.gov/frsp/interns.htm
Phone: (540) 373–6124

Description/Positions Available: Located 50 miles south of Washington, D.C. and 50 miles north of Richmond, Virginia, Fredericksburg and Spotsylvania National Military Park comprises 8,000 acres preserving four major Civil War battlefields—Fredericksburg, Chancellorsville, the Wilderness, and Spotsylvania Court House.

Historical Interpreters are needed for the spring, summer, and fall. Volunteers in this position assist park visitors to plan their stay and research and answer historical questions. Some volunteers receive additional training and conduct guided walking tours over the battlefields. Housing is normally available, and mileage reimbursement and a meals stipend provided. While the Historical Interpreters comprise the largest volunteer program in the park, we have also had volunteers in the positions of Curatorial Assistant, Historical Researcher, Cultural Resource Management Assistant, Structural Restoration Assistant, and Education Program Assistant in the past.

James River Ranger District, George Washington and Jefferson National Forests

Agency: U.S. Department of Agriculture Forest Service
Season: Summer
Contact: Sharon Mohney
810a Madison Ave.
Covington, VA 24426
E-mail: smohney@fs.fed.us
Web: www.southernregion.fs.fed.us/gwj/

developedrecareas.htm

Phone: (540) 962–2214

Description/Positions Available: The fifty-five-site Morris Hill Campground is part of a larger recreation area adjacent to the 2,300-acre Lake Moomaw, nestled in the Allegheny Mountains of Virginia. The campsites are not adjacent to the lake but are within walking distance. The nearby Coles Point Recreation Area has a swimming beach, bathhouse, picnic shelters, and boat ramp; the Fortney Branch boat ramp is also nearby. Lake Moomaw is stocked with trout, bass, pickerel, and perch. Two campsites with full hookups, suitable for RVs, are available for Volunteer Campground Hosts, and are located adjacent to bathhouses with hot showers.

Campground Hosts live on site, providing information to campers and staffing the Visitors Center for four to five days per week. Other duties include light maintenance, opening and closing bathhouses, and monitoring payment compliance. Depending on the volunteers' interests and abilities, they might do interpretive presentations, hikes, etc. We can accept couples or singles at each Host campsite. W prefer people who can stay from May to September, but can accommodate shorter durations. Pets must be leashed at all times, and cannot go inside the Visitors Center.

Mount Rogers National Recreation Area

Agency: U.S. Department of Agriculture Forest Service
Season: Year-round
Contact: Doug Byerly, Volunteer Coordinator
3714 Hwy. 16
Marion, VA 24354
E-mail: dbyerly@fs.fed.us
Web: www.southernregion.fs.fed.us/gwj
Phone: (276) 782–4374 or (800) 628–7202

Description/Positions Available: Located in the mountains of southwest Virginia along the Tennessee and North Carolina borders, the Mount Rogers National Recreation Area fea-tures more than 400 miles of trails including the Appalachian Trail, eleven campgrounds, three designated wilderness areas, four visitor centers and the highest mountain in the state of Virginia. Various lodging accommodations and a stipend of $10 per workday are usually provided. Dates are flexible for all positions, but there are more opportunities in the spring, summer, and fall. We request a commitment of at least one month of service.

Be a Backcountry Ranger. Your duties will include performing general trail and trailhead maintenance, making visitor contacts, educating visitors about zero-impact techniques, and collecting visitor use data in the mountain crest zone and designated wilderness areas. The work schedule is ten days in the backcountry and four days off. How about becoming a Mountain Bike Trail Ranger? Your duties include patrolling the Virginia Creeper Trail, a 34-mile National Recreation Trail, on a mountain bike (provided), making visitor contacts, performing general trail and trailhead maintenance, educating visitors about zero-impact outdoor ethics, and maintaining informational bulletin boards. Volunteers will work alone most of the time. Trail Maintenance Crew Leaders are also needed. Volunteers will lead several Volunteer Trail Crews for one- to three-week periods. Duties include coordinating and supervising the assigned work projects, performing and teaching general trail maintenance, transporting crews, shopping for food, and organizing work assignments at the base camp. Visitor Center Staff and Interpretive Programming Volunteers will be offered positions rotating between four unique visitor centers. Duties include interacting with the public, providing visitors with information in person and on the telephone, presenting interpretive programs in campgrounds and visitor centers, and preparing interpretive materials for bulletin boards and brochures. Finally, we need an Environmental Educator. The responsibilities of this job include visiting local schools, organized groups and events such as festivals and fairs to increase environmental awareness and to teach outdoor ethics. Several ready-to-use programs are available.

Prince William Forest Park

Agency: National Park Service
Season: Year-round
Contact: David Elkowitz
18100 Park Headquarters Rd.
Triangle, VA 22172
E-mail: David_Elkowitz@nps.gov
Web: www.nps.gov/prwi
Phone: (703) 730–7264

Description/Positions Available: Prince William Forest Park is a 17,000-or-more-acre park preserving a variety of natural and cultural history within 32 miles of Washington, D.C. The park has 37 miles of hiking trails, or more miles of mountain bike trails, and numerous cultural opportunities varying from CCC cabins to the OSS.

Take part in our Adopt-A-Trail Volunteer program. Your duties will include using hand tools (shovels, Pulaskis, pruning shears, etc.) in repairing erosion controls, delineating trails, eliminating short-cut trails, constructing/repairing boardwalk, removing vegetation covering trails, inspecting/repairing trail signs, and litter pickup. Also, there is a need for general trail patrol and inspection.

Richmond National Battlefield Park

Agency: National Park Service
Season: Year-round
Contact: Edward P. Sanders
3215 East Broad St.
Richmond, VA 23223
E-mail: Ed_Sanders@nps.gov
Web: www.nps.gov/rich
Phone: (804) 226–1981

Description/Positions Available: Commemorating several decisive battles of the Civil War, this park features the Richmond of the 1860s mingled with modern Richmond and provides a fascinating perspective on our nation's history.

A Visitor Center Interpreter is needed to staff the information desk.

Washington

Chelan Ranger District, Wenatchee National Forest

Agency: U.S. Department of Agriculture Forest Service
Season: Summer
Contact: Ken Dull
428 W. Woodin Ave.
Chelan, WA 98831
E-mail: kjdull@fs.fed.us
Web: www.fs.fed.us/r6/wenatchee/
Phone: (509) 682–2576

Description/Positions Available: Glacier Peak Wilderness accessed via Lake Chelan. The only way to get to Glacier Peak Wilderness on the Chelan Ranger District is to take a boat for 20 or 30 miles up Lake Chelan. At the end of the boat ride, shuttle buses provide rides up either Railroad Creek Valley on the Chelan Ranger District or the Stehekin River Valley in the North Cascade National Park Complex. These volunteer positions are located in the Railroad Creek Valley, where the shuttle bus ride ends at Holden Village, a deserted company mining village that has been converted to a Christian retreat center and has a summer population of 400. The Glacier Peak Wilderness borders Holden Village on three sides, and there are several wilderness trails that originate from here. Copper Basin, Holden Lake, and Hart Lake are wilderness destinations that are popular day hikes from Holden Village. Beyond Hart Lake, a trail continues on up the Railroad Creek Valley past Lyman Lake, over Cloudy Pass, and down into Agnes Creek where it joins the Pacific Crest National Scenic Trail. The Lake Chelan, Railroad Creek, and Agnes Creek

Valleys are extremely deep glaciated valleys carved out by alpine and continental glaciers. Above the Railroad Creek Valley on the north side is Bonaza Peak, the highest non-volcanic peak in the North Cascades, and on the south side is a chain of peaks that form the highest continuous ridge of peaks in the North Cascades. There are still many active glaciers in the high mountain cirques such as Holden Lake and Upper Lyman Lake. The North Cascades Mountains are known as the "Alps" of North America. Beyond the few major trails, travel through this portion of the North Cascades is restricted to mountaineers.

We have two positions for Volunteer Wilderness Rangers. One is based out of Holden Village, and the second is based out of a ranger camp at Lyman Lake. Both positions involve contacting visitors on wilderness trails, sharing wilderness education topics with the visitors, and assisting with trail maintenance that requires the use of handtools. The positions are for two to three months with a work schedule of ten days on followed by four days off. Both positions come with a per diem of $15, and transportation to and from the District Office, uniforms, radios, and camping gear are all provided. However, applicants must provide their own vehicle for transportation when out of the mountains on days off. Become a Holder Ranger! Most of the hiking required is day hiking, with the opportunity for a short backpacking trip or two. In addition to working in the wilderness, there is the opportunity to work with the Holden Village Hike Haus staff in putting on a wilderness zero-impact program once a week in the Village. This involves presenting a slide program to groups of twenty to thirty people. Some maintenance of a small campground with two sites is also part of this position. Housing is provided at a Forest Service cabin and campsite that is a five-minute walk from the Village. The cabin has a kitchen with running cold water, wood and electric stoves, refrigerator, food storage areas, and office space. The "bedroom" is a tent (provided) located in a site next to the cabin. At times, the cabin is shared with other Forest Service employees, such as the Lyman Lake volunteer and the Wilderness Trail Rangers. Hot showers, sauna, washing machine, and ice-cream snack bar are available in the Village. Prepared meals may also be purchased and enjoyed at the Village dining hall. Get involved at Lyman Lake. Backpacking the 8 miles between Holden Village and the ranger camp at Lyman Lake is required every ten-day work period. Most of the work will be done on day hikes out of the ranger camp. The camp has a large tent for kitchen and office space, a separate tent as the "bedroom," and a Wallowa toilet. The large tent is occasionally shared with other wilderness rangers. There will be several short backpacking trips away from the base camp into Agnes Creek.

Cispus Learning Center

Agency: NON PRO
Season: Year-round
Contact: Martin E. Fortin, Jr.
2142 Cispus Rd.
Randle, WA 98377
E-mail: cispuslc@cispus.org
Web: www.cispus.org

Description/Positions Available: We run an outdoor education facility for up to 400. It is located in the Gifford Pinchot National Forest, centered between Mount St. Helens, Mount Rainier, and Mount Adams.

Interns are needed for environmental education curriculum development and for challenge course.

Colville National Forest

Agency: U.S. Department of Agriculture Forest Service
Season: Summer
Contact: Keith Wakefield
180 N. Jefferson
Republic, WA 99166
E-mail: kwakefield@fs.fed.us
Web: www.fs.fed.us/r6/colville/
Phone: (509) 775–7400

Description/Positions Available: N.E. Washington, Republic Ranger District, Republic Washington, Kettle Range Trails.

Trail volunteers, Campground Hosts, interpretive Program Leaders, and Adopt-a-Trail Volunteers are all needed.

Gifford Pinchot National Forest

Agency: U.S. Department of Agriculture Forest Service
Season: Year-round
Contact: Kristi Cochrane
Coldwater Ridge Visitor Center Mp43/ 3029 Spirit Lake Hwy.
Castle Rock , WA 98611
E-mail: kcochran@fs.fed.us
Web: www.fs.fed.us/gpnf/mshnvm
Phone: (360) 274–2131

Description/Positions Available: Be a Volcano Volunteer at Mount St. Helens! Spend at least twelve weeks helping visitors gain an understanding of the geologic and biologic processes that have shaped this National Volcanic Monument. If you enjoy learning, sharing information with the public, giving talks, providing guided walks, talking with visitors while roving trails, and assisting Forest Service staff with day-to-day Visitor Center operations, then this is the volunteer opportunity for you. Come experience and be a part of this ever-changing landscape as a Volcano Volunteer. The Forest Service provides volunteers with bunkhouse-style housing, a small daily stipend, a variety of in-depth training opportunities, and uniforms. Enthusiastic individuals, who are willing to perform a multitude of different tasks, are needed.

Gifford Pinchot National Forest, Mount Adams Ranger District

Agency: U.S. Department of Agriculture Forest Service

Season: Summer
Contact: Ross J. Bluestone
2455 Hwy. 141
Trout Lake, WA 98650
E-mail: rbluestone@fs.fed.us
Web: www.fs.fed.us/gpnf/
Phone: (509) 395–3354

Description/Positions Available: Southwest Washington State, North of Columbia River, Southern Washington Cascades.

Trail Maintenance helpers are needed from June through Labor Day; Information Reception helpers are required year-round.

Lake Roosevelt National Recreation Area

Agency: National Park Service
Season: Spring to fall
Contact: Lynn Brougher
1008 Crest Dr.
Coulee Dam, WA 99116
Web: www.nps.gov/laro/home.htm
Phone: (509) 633–9441, extension 130

Description/Positions Available: Lake Roosevelt stretches for 150 miles to the Canadian border in mountainous northeastern Washington State. Natural wonders like the Grand Coulee, the world's largest flood-carved canyon, are complemented by cultural riches that include one of the greatest concentrations of archaeological sites in the northwest.

Interpretive Aides are needed to assist with guided canoe trips, living-history programs, watershed-education activities on a floating classroom, and visitor center duties. Benefits include training, supervision, and housing. Campground Hosts are needed to assist in campground management at sites along Lake Roosevelt. Applicants must have their own RV/camper, but hookups are provided.

Mount Baker–Snoqualmie National Forest

Agency: U.S. Department of Agriculture Forest Service
Season: Summer
Contact: Mary Ann Coughlin
450 Roosevelt Ave. N.
Enumclaw, WA 98022
E-mail: mcoughlin@fs.fed.us
Web: www.fs.fed.us/r6/mbs/
Phone: (360) 825–6586

Description/Positions Available: Norse Peak and Clearwater Wilderness.

Patrol, maintain, educate and enforce wilderness rules and ethics. Volunteers must be physically fit and moderately experienced backpackers. Housing and a stipend are available. Two to four positions are available between late May and late September (flexible).

Mount Rainier National Park

Agency: National Park Service
Season: Year-round
Contact: Volunteers-In-Parks Coordinator
Tahoma Woods, Star Rte.
Ashford, WA 98304
E-mail: mora_vips@nps.gov
Web: www.nps.gov/mora

Description/Positions Available: We are located in Western Washington State, two hours south of Seattle.

We have opportunities for a wide variety of volunteers. Please see our Web site for current details. The majority of our volunteers work from June until the beginning of September.

Mount St. Helens National Volcanic Monument

Agency: U.S. Department of Agriculture Forest Service
Season: Summer
Contact: Hans Castren

42218 N.E. Yale Bridge Rd.
Amboy, WA 98601
E-mail: Hans_castren@fs.fed.us
Web: www.fs.fed.us/gpnf
Phone: (360) 247–3900

Description/Positions Available: We need volunteers for backcountry climbing rangers. Uniforms are required and provided.

Mount St. Helens National Volcanic Monument

Agency: U.S. Department of Agriculture Forest Service
Season: Summer
Contact: Al Conaway
42218 N.E. Yale Bridge Rd.
Amboy, WA 98601
E-mail: aconaway@fs.fed.us
Web: www.fs.fed.us/gpnf
Phone: (360) 247–3900

Description/Positions Available: On the south side of the mountain. Mount St. Helens NVM work station at Pine Creek is located 20 miles north of Vancouver, Washington, and 47 miles east of Woodland, Washington, on state highway 503/Forest Road 90. The site also contains an information station and NWIA bookstore. Government housing or motor-home/trailer hookups possibly may also be available on site.

Four people are needed to operate the information station (one or two people will be on duty at any given time). We want to have an information station open between 9:00 A.M. and 6:00 P.M. daily to give information on road condition, places to see, things to do, sale passes, maps, and books.

Mount St. Helens National Volcanic Monument

Agency: U.S. Department of Agriculture Forest Service
Season: Summer
Contact: Al Conaway

42218 N.E. Yale Bridge Rd.
Amboy, WA 98601
E-mail: aconaway@fs.fed.us/gpnf
Web: www.fs.fed.us/gpnf
Phone: (360) 247–3900

Description/Positions Available: Pine Creek Information Station is located 19 miles east of Cougar, Washington on Forest Road 90 in the Gifford Pinchot National Forest.

Visitor Information Assistants are needed. Individuals will provide forest visitors with information about Mount St. Helens and the surrounding area. The information station contains a small theater, book sales area, and information desk. Some cashiering may be required. Days/hours are negotiable; housing/stipend may be possible.

Okanogan-Wenatchee National Forest

Agency: U.S. Department of Agriculture Forest Service
Season: Summer
Contact: Jennifer Zbyszewski
P.O. Box 188
Twisp, WA 98856
E-mail: jzbyszewski@fs.fed.us
Web: www.fs.fed.us/r6/wenatchee/

Description/Positions Available: The Methow Valley Ranger District, Okanogan-Wenatchee National Forest is located on the east side of the North Cascades. The North Cascades Scenic Corridor runs east to west through the North Cascades range. Trails access high lakes and mountain passes along the corridor. Twisp and Winthrop, small towns in the Methow Valley, provide most services and a variety of recreational opportunities.

A Front Country Ranger is required for hiking trails in the North Cascades Scenic Area. Duties may include educating and providing information to the public, cleaning up campsites, collecting use and site information, and light trail maintenance. Hiking experience, good physical health,

and communication skills are all necessary. The work will primarily involve day hikes with a few short backpacking trips. A stipend and housing may be available. Uniforms, training, and some equipment will be provided.

Okanogan-Wenatchee National Forest

Agency: U.S. Department of Agriculture Forest Service
Season: Summer
Contact: Laurie Dowie
P.O. Box 188
Twisp, WA 98856
E-mail: ldowie@fs.fed.us
Web: www.fs.fed.us/r6/wenatchee/
Phone: (509) 997–9771

Description/Positions Available: The Methow Valley Ranger District, Okanogan-Wenatchee National Forest, is located on the east side of the North Cascades. The Pasayten and Lake Chelan "Sawtooth" wildernesses encompass more than 700,000 acres and are bordered by the North Cascades National Park and Recreation Area. The terrain ranges from glaciated peaks and high lakes to rolling meadows and forest. Twisp and Winthrop, two small towns in the Methow Valley, provide most services. Recreational opportunities are diverse with mountain biking, rafting, and kayaking available as well as hiking.

One or two people are needed to produce an inventory of campsites/conditions and campsite rehabilitation in the Pasayten and Lake Chelan-Sawtooth Wildernesses. Backpacking skills and experience are essential as trips can extend up to ten days. GPS/GIS skills would be helpful but not mandatory. A stipend and housing may be available. Uniforms, training, and some equipment are provided.

Olympic National Forest

Agency: U.S. Department of Agriculture Forest Service

Season: Summer

Contact: Molly Erickson

437 Tillicum Lane

Forks, WA 98331

E-mail: mjerickson@fs.fed.us

Web: www.fs.fed.us/r6/olympic

Phone: (360) 374–1233

Description/Positions Available: We are located in the Sol Duc Valley, in the heart of the Northwest Olympic Peninsula between the Pacific Ocean, the Hoh Rain Forest, Lake Crescent, and the Olympic Mountains. The area is just west of Forks, and Port Angeles is 50 miles to the east.

We have several opportunities for folks who would like to volunteer. These include becoming a Campground Host at Klahanie Campground—a Level II rustic camp area that is just being reopened—or an Interpretive guide for fire lookout, historic, and natural resource programs. You could also become part of a future GIS projects.

Olympic National Forest, Hood Canal District

Agency: U.S. Department of Agriculture Forest Service

Season: Summer

Contact: Steve Ricketts or Susie Graham

P.O. Box 280

Quilcene, WA 98376

Web: www.fs.fed.us/r6/olympic

Phone: (360) 765–2200

Description/Positions Available: Located on the eastern side of the Olympic Peninsula, the district is known for its lakes, rivers, and Olympic Mountain peaks. The district office is in Quilcene with a work center in Hoodsport. The district manages four wildernesses, fifteen campgrounds, more than 200 miles of trail, and many other dispersed recreation areas.

A Campground Host is needed from May 1 to September 15 at Wynoochee Lake. Electricity and water are both available, and there is a dump station nearby. This is a remote, but popular, site

approximately 35 miles north of the community of Montesano, Washington, over a rough gravel road. We need people able to commit for the whole summer. Recreation Area Hosts are needed between May 15 and October 1 for Skokomish River Recreation Areas to provide information to the public and to work with the recreation crew on area beautification and maintenance. Applicants will need their own trailer and vehicle. Full hookups are provided. A Campground Host is also needed, this time from July 15 to September 15 at Seal Rock Campground. Full hookups are again available. This is a popular salt-water oyster beach on Hood Canal located approximately 1 mile north of the small community of Brinnon on U.S. 101.

Olympic National Forest, Quilcene District

Agency: U.S. Department of Agriculture Forest Service

Season: Spring to fall

Contact: Steve Ricketts

P.O. Box 280

Quilcene, WA 98376

Phone: (360) 765–2227

Description/Positions Available: Located on the northeast corner of the Olympic Peninsula in the rain shadow of the Olympic Mountains, this district is bordered to the west by Olympic National Park and to the east by Hood Canal and Puget Sound. Six campgrounds, more than 100 miles of trails and the 44,258-acre Buckhorn Wilderness are included within its boundaries. The terrain rises from sea level up to 7,134 feet and supports a variety of ecosystems.

Campground Hosts are needed from May to October in three campgrounds. Amenities range from full hookups to hand-pump wells and vault toilets. Trail Crew Workers and a Wilderness Ranger are needed to help maintain district trails and to assist with backcountry patrols, public contact, and resource-management projects. Trails vary from multi-use to primitive. Duties usually involve overnight stays and weekends. Benefits possibly include per diem, equipment and bunkhouse on first-come, first-served basis. An Interpretive/Naturalist is needed to conduct walks in a seashore/marine setting, lead evening talks and viewpoint programs, and develop information displays. Benefits possibly include per diem, uniform, and bunkhouse. Finally, we have an opening for a Maintenance Worker to perform light cleaning of campground facilities and aid in facility repair and construction.

Olympic National Park

Agency: National Park Service
Season: Year-round
Contact: Maurie Sprague
600 E. Park Ave.
Port Angeles, WA 98362
E-mail: maurie_sprague@nps.gov
Web: www.nps.gov/olym
Phone: (360) 565–3141

Description/Positions Available: This park is a magnificently diversified area that features glaciated peaks, alpine meadows, broad valleys, sparkling lakes and rivers, temperate rain forest and 57 miles of spectacular Pacific Ocean coastline offering tremendous recreational opportunities.

Campground Hosts are needed for the summer only. Applicants require their own trailers, but a site with water, electricity, and possibly septic hookups will be provided. Information Assistants are needed year-round to staff visitor centers and assist with special projects. Revegetation/Backcountry Rangers are also needed to assist in a variety of projects. Benefits include training, some type of housing, and college credit by arrangement. Mid-June to Labor Day recommended time frame. Education Ranger Interns are being recruited to work as entry level interpretive rangers alongside an experienced ranger as well as independently. Winter interns conduct walks on snowshoe at Hurricane Ridge between March and early June. Wilderness Resources/Revegetation officers have a variety of responsibilities relating to the management of the 877,000 acres wilderness. This post requires excellent physical condition, a willing-

ness to work in soggy, cool weather conditions, and adaptability and the ability to work closely with others. Field season in the mountains is short because of snow cover, and there is an abundance of work to complete in fall. You should expect to spend 50 percent of your time in the wilderness. The rest will be in greenhouses and the resource office in Port Angeles. Mid-June to late September are the dates of the position, though applicants willing to continue until late October are preferred. Wilderness Information Center Assistants are also needed. Your role will be to provide wilderness information, camping permits, and reservations. You must be familiar directly or indirectly with Olympic's wilderness. This position is intended for those willing to commit to it for twelve weeks or more, full-time, between late April and mid-September.

Olympic National Park

Agency: National Park Service
Season: June to October
Contact: Ruth Scott
600 East Park Ave.
Port Angeles, WA 98362
E-mail: ruth_scott@nps.gov

Description/Positions Available: Olympic National Park is an incredibly diverse national park located on the Olympic Peninsula in northwestern Washington State. Known for its old-growth temperate rainforests, it is also graced with subalpine meadows and lake-basins, glacier-covered mountain peaks, and the largest remaining portion of wild coastline in the contiguous United States. In 1988, 95 percent of the park was designated as the Olympic Wilderness, "to secure for the American people of present and future generations the benefits of an enduring resource of wilderness."

Wilderness Resources Internships are available and require a minimum commitment of four months. The field season in the Olympic Mountains is short because of late seasonal snowmelt and early autumn snowfall. There is an abundance of work to complete during this short window so dates of availability, especially in the fall months, are a key screening criterion. It is important that interns be available for work through at least mid-October. Interested interns can begin earlier or stay later as well. Experience with hiking/backpacking, and gardening or greenhouse work is desirable but not mandatory. It is imperative, however, that interns be in excellent physical condition, are able to hike over rough terrain with a loaded backpack, and willing to work in soggy, cool weather conditions. Interns also need to be able to live and work closely with a crew of employees and other volunteer/interns. Park volunteers are provided with shared housing in government quarters, located 5 miles from the town of Port Angeles. In addition, a stipend of $100 per month is provided during their stay. Transportation to and from trailheads is provided. A personal vehicle provides more flexibility on days off.

San Juan Island National Historical Park

Agency: National Park Service
Season: Summer
Contact: Mike Vouri
P.O. Box 429
Friday Harbor, WA 98250
E-mail: mike_vouri@nps.gov
Web: www.nps.gov/sajh/home.htm

Description/Positions Available: San Juan Island NHP, which commemorates the peaceful resolution of the 1846–1872 water boundary dispute between Great Britain and the United States, is located on San Juan Island, one of a cluster of emerald islands in Puget Sound accessible by the Washington State ferry system. This park features spectacular island and mountain scenery. Forest, prairie and coastal environments provide opportunities for hiking, birding, whale-watching and marine recreation.

Information Assistants are needed year-round to staff visitor centers and work on special projects. Living History Re-Enactors are also being

recruited. They wear 1860s military uniforms and costumes to act out camp life at American and English camps. History/Natural History Interpreters are also needed to conduct research and public-education activities. Gardener Interpreters are needed to maintain and interpret the formal garden. We are also looking for Resource Management Assistants to maintain trails, help eradicate nonnative plants, and assist with varied fire- and vegetation-management projects. Benefits include training and college credit by arrangement.

Umatilla National Forest Walla Walla Ranger District

Agency: U.S. Department of Agriculture Forest Service
Season: Summer
Contact: Jeff Bloom, Recreation Specialist
1415 W. Rose St.
Walla Walla, WA 99362
E-mail: jbloom@fs.fed.us
Web: www.fs.fed.us/r6/uma/
Phone: (509) 522–6277

Description/Positions Available: Umatilla Forks Campground in northeast Oregon, 33 miles east of Pendleton. The site's elevation is 2200 feet, and it is adjacent to North Fork Umatilla Wilderness. Umatilla River provides catch and release fishing. Access is via paved roads except for the last 4 miles of generally good gravel. Season is from Memorial Day weekend to Labor Day weekend, five days per week. Days off fall midweek. You will be provided with a $15 per diem subsistence, plus reimbursement for propane. The campsite is provided with a water hookup but unfortunately full hookups are not available.

Duties include greeting campers, explaining regulations, doing minor maintenance, cleaning campsites, and keeping toilets clean and serviceable. There are fifteen sites and we require one Host; single women are not recommended by the agency.

Washington State Parks

Agency: State parks
Season: Year-round
Contact: Volunteer Programs
P.O. Box 42650
Olympia, WA 98504
E-mail: sarah.oldfield@parks.wa.gov
Web: www.parks.wa.gov
Phone: (360) 902–8583

Description/Positions Available: Experience the many diverse climates of Washington by volunteering in the 125 camping and day-use state parks. Ninety percent have full hookups along with cell phones for month-long stays for hosts or volunteers. Individuals and groups are encouraged to volunteer on a one-time or continuing basis. Adopt-a-park program is available for groups performing a continuous service twice a year every year. Interested person(s) can directly contact the park for projects or be on an emergency call list for service. Parks are part of the local community and can use local citizens help on many different levels. Volunteers are a critical part of our state agency and recognized as such. Thank you for your interest in working with our state park system!

We especially need Hosts for campgrounds, interpretive centers, marine parks, and Environmental Learning Centers used by groups. Also, volunteers are required to assist park staff with carpentry, electrical, plumbing/sewer, mechanical, and painting. Your services would also be useful in providing general maintenance/cleanup, trail maintenance, computer operation, environmental programs, flora/fauna identification, historical park research, interpretive assistance, office assistance, and photography.

Washington Trails Association and Olympic National Park

Agency: National Park Service
Season: Spring
Contact: Jan Klippert

14036 Meridian Ave. N.
Seattle, WA 98133
E-mail: jpklippert@aol.com
Phone: (206) 364–2689

Description/Positions Available: Volunteers collect and remove marine generated debris from 60 miles of Olympic National Park Pacific Ocean beaches during the April 20, 2002, weekend. twenty miles of the beach are easily accessible by car or one day hike. The remaining 40 miles require backpacking and zero-impact camping skills.

We are looking for volunteers to collect and help remove debris from the beaches.

Whitman Mission National Historic Site

Agency: National Park Service
Season: Year-round
Contact: Volunteer Coordinator
328 Whitman Mission Rd.
Walla Walla, WA 99362
Phone: (509) 522–6360

Description/Positions Available: Retired people and college students are needed year-round. Several programs provide volunteers with a wide range of opportunities and allow them to develop skills and gain experience working with people.

Curatorial duties include the computerized cataloging of artifacts and historical research. Interpretation duties include research, photography, special events, talks, and demonstrating 1840s costumes, skills and crafts. Maintenance duties include groundskeeping, painting, designing and maintaining flowerbeds, small engine maintenance, and basic carpentry. No housing is provided. The nearest housing is located in Walla Walla, 7 miles from the job site. Benefits include mileage reimbursement to and from Walla Walla, college credit by arrangement, and computer training.

West Virginia

Harpers Ferry National Historical Park

Agency: National Park Service
Season: Year-round
Contact: David Fox
P.O. Box 65
Harpers Ferry, WV 25425
E-mail: david_fox@nps.gov
Web: www.nps.gov/hafe

Description/Positions Available: History and nature come together here in the shadow of the Blue Ridge Mountains where the Shenandoah River flows into the Potomac. The Appalachian Trail intersects the Chesapeake & Ohio Canal at this nationally significant site. Washington, D.C., is accessible by commuter train.

Volunteer and intern opportunities Include Information Services, Historian, Archeologist, Curator, Library Assistant, and Gardener. Housing and an RV pad are available.

Monongahela National Forest, Potomac District

Agency: U.S. Department of Agriculture Forest Service
Season: Spring to fall
Contact: Volunteer Coordinator
HC 59 Box 240
Petersburg, WV 26847
Phone: (304) 257–4488

Description/Positions Available: Independent and reliable volunteers are needed to work on Trail Maintenance Crews, to serve as Campground Hosts, and to work as Interpreters and Naturalists. All positions require working weekends and the ability to drive. Benefits may include housing or trailer space and subsistence pay. Six- to ten-week commitments are preferred.

West Virginia Scenic Trails Association

Agency: NON PRO
Season: Summer
Contact: Doug Wood
HC 65, Box 182
Forest Hill, WV 24935
E-mail: CHINGWE@peoplepc.com
Web: www.wvonline.com/wvsta/
Phone: (304) 466–2724

Description/Positions Available: Allegheny Trail in Monongahela, George Washington, and Jefferson National Forests. This long-distance footpath traverses the Allegheny Highlands of West Virginia and the north and south of Virginia. Some portions of the trail are in southern red spruce forests, others in northern hardwood, and others in oak/pine/hickory forests. Remote hiking opportunities abound as do fishing, hunting, and wildlife watching pleasures.

Volunteer laborers are needed for Wood's Wacky Week of Work and Welaxation. This falls in the week of June 20, 2002. Mid-week duties include a tour of historical/cultural/natural points of interest in the area adjacent to the work sites. We are looking for several worker skills, including branch pruning, sawyers, paint blazers, tread constructors, shelter/bridge carpenters, cooks, storytellers, singers and all-around nice outdoor folks. Camping skills and personal equipment are required.

Wisconsin

Apostle Islands National Lakeshore

Agency: National Park Service
Season: Summer
Contact: Margaret Ludwig
Rte. 1, Box 4
Bayfield, WI 54814
Phone: (715) 779–3397, extension 105

Description/Positions Available: The twenty-one islands of Lake Superior off the northern tip of Wisconsin offer hiking and camping in a true wilderness setting and also are home to a cultural history that includes lighthouses, fish camps, stone quarries, and logging camps.

Lighthouse Keepers are needed for a minimum of three months. Keepers will live in historic structure, mow lawns, and greet occasional visitors. Campground Hosts are also needed for a small primitive campground located on the islands. The minimum period of commitment required is two months.

Chequamegon National Forest, Washburn District

Agency: U.S. Department of Agriculture Forest Service
Season: Summer
Contact: Phil Freeman
113 E Bayfield St.
Washburn, WI 54891
Phone: (715) 373–2667

Description/Positions Available: Located in northwestern Wisconsin, recreation opportunities abound in our area. These include hiking, camping, hunting, mountain biking, and ATV riding, as well as water-based activities such as sea-kayaking and fishing on both inland lakes and Lake Superior.

A Wilderness Sentinel is needed to gather visitor-use information and perform trail maintenance. Subsistence may be available. Campground Hosts are also needed at two locations. Your duties will include doing general campground maintenance, providing customer information, and ensuring all are aware of campground rules. Subsistence may be available. Campgrounds include: Birch Grove Campground, a sixteen-site primitive campground. It is located between and on the shores of two small lakes which produce a tranquil environment. Horseshoe Lake Campground is found in the central part of the Bayfield Peninsula. It has eleven campsites and trailhead parking. The campground is designed for riders and their horses with hitching rails at each site and longer, drive-through parking for vehicles and horse trailers.

Chequamegon-Nicolet National Forest

Agency: U.S. Department of Agriculture Forest Service
Season: Summer
Contact: Dawn M Meier
850 N. 8th St.
Medford, WI 54451
E-mail: dmeier@fs.fed.us
Phone: (715) 748–4875, extension 43

Description/Positions Available: Located northwest of Medford, this 121,488-acre district offers camping, fishing, hiking, hunting, skiing, picnicking, and other dispersed recreation. Characterized by gently rolling terrain, the sparsely populated rural region offers an opportunity to escape from urban living.

People interested in natural resources, recreation, wildlife or forestry can gain valuable experience and training. Free camping is available for Campground Hosts, who will welcome visitors and provide local information between May and

September. Trail Crews are needed to work on maintenance projects on a 49-mile section of the Ice Age National Scenic Trail.

Dane County Parks

Agency: State parks
Season: Summer
Contact: Louise Goldstein
4318 Robertson Rd.
Madison, WI 53714
E-mail: goldstein@co.dane.wi.us
Web: www.co.dane.wi.us/parks/adult/adult.html

Situated in south central Wisconsin, this area offers many outdoor recreational opportunities. The county abounds in sparkling lakes and waterways, natural areas, and trails. It is the home of the University of Wisconsin and the state capital in Madison and provides many cultural, recreational, and entertainment opportunities.

Volunteer Campground Hosts are needed from May 1 to the end of October. Hosts live at the park for a minimum of four weeks, provide hospitality and information to campers, serve as liaisons to staff and perform light maintenance. Campsite, electricity, training, and supervision are provided. You must be friendly, easy-going, and a good camping role model. Must provide personal references, your own camper/RV, and personal communication device. Water and dump facilities are available at two campgrounds, full hookup at three.

Necedah National Wildlife Refuge

Agency: U.S. Fish and Wildlife Service
Season: Year-round
Contact: Jennifer Rabuck
W7996 20th St. W.
Necedah, WI 54646
E-mail: jennifer_rabuck@fws.gov
Web: www.fws.gov/r3pao/necedah/
Phone: (608) 565–4412

Description/Positions Available: Located in Central Wisconsin, this 44,000-acre refuge is home to the world's largest population of endangered Karner blue butterflies, the southern-most pack of timber wolves in Wisconsin and is the reintroduction site for the eastern migratory flock of whooping cranes. The refuge is predominantly wetlands with sandy savanna ridges. Free housing is available to volunteers!

Naturalist(s) are needed to work with groups, including school parties, and the general public. You will also be required to assist with events, information dispersal, trails, leaflets, and signage. Public Information Aide(s) are needed for reception and office work, data entry, and visitor relations. Biology Aide(s) will assist with tracking surveys, population counts, and botany research. Maintenance Assistant(s) are required to assist with painting, carpentry, repairs, and landscaping.

Nicolet National Forest, Eagle River and Florence Districts

Agency: U.S. Department of Agriculture Forest Service
Season: June to August
Contact: Jeff Herrett
P.O. Box 1809
Eagle River, WI 54521
Phone: (715) 479–2827

Description/Positions Available: Numerous lakes and rivers surrounded by pine and hardwood forests in this ranger district attract many summer visitors. Fishing, canoeing, hiking, mountain bicycling, and camping opportunities abound. The town of Eagle River is a popular vacation destination. The town of Florence is home to the Wild Rivers Interpretive Center.

Recreation/Trails/Wilderness Interns or Volunteers are needed to assist with the operation and maintenance of fourteen campgrounds and associated facilities. These positions will also help to maintain trails and three designated wilderness areas. Public contact skills are necessary. You will be provided with a stipend of $30 per working day, uniform, and free government housing. On-duty time for research and preparation of college-credit intern projects is negotiable. Interns are responsible for arranging for-credit projects with the university. The intern or volunteer will be on duty for a total of eighty hours every two weeks. Campground Hosts needed to welcome visitors, answer questions, and perform some light maintenance. Free camping is provided. Peak demand is for the period of June to August.

Nicolet National Forest, Lakewood/Laona District

Agency: U.S. Department of Agriculture Forest Service
Season: June to September
Contact: Darrell Richards
4978 Hwy. 8 W.
Laona, WI 54541
Phone: (715) 674–4481

Description/Positions Available: Spend a summer in beautiful northeastern Wisconsin and enjoy great stream and lake fishing, hiking,

camping, and canoeing.

A Campground Host is needed to assist the public, dispense information, and perform light cleanup duties between June and September. Free campsite space is provided.

Wisconsin Department of Natural Resources

Agency: State parks
Season: Summer
Contact: Mark Brandt
Box 7921
Madison, WI 53707
Web: www.dnr.state.wi.us/
Phone: (608) 264–6042

Description/Positions Available: Wisconsin has abundant trails and more than seventy state parks, forests, and recreation areas with terrain ranging from flat to rolling hills.

Campground Hosts are needed at forty-five state parks and forests. Other volunteers are needed for Trail Maintenance, Patrolling, Interpretive Work, and other special projects.

Wyoming

Bridger-Teton National Forest, Big Piney District

Agency: U.S. Department of Agriculture Forest Service
Season: Summer
Contact: John Haugh
P.O. Box 218
Big Piney, WY 83113
E-mail: Jhaugh@fs.fed.us
Phone: (307) 739–5213 or (307) 276–3375

Description/Positions Available: This district is located in southwestern Wyoming approximately 90 miles south of Jackson Hole. The Wyoming Range dominates the district and offers outstanding dispersed camping and non-

wilderness hiking on trails that receive little public use.

Volunteers are needed to perform Trail Maintenance, Backcountry Patrol, Dispersed-Site Management, and Trailhead Construction and Maintenance. Stock-handling and backcountry-camping skills are preferred. Benefits may include housing and subsistence.

Bureau of Land Management Lander Field Office

Agency: Bureau of Land Management
Season: Summer
Contact: Gary Long
P.O. Box 589

Lander, WY 82520
E-mail: Gary_Long@blm.gov
Web: www.wy.blm.gov
Phone: (307) 332–8407

Description/Positions Available: We operate the Atlantic City/Big Atlantic Gulch Campgrounds 30 miles southwest of Lander, Wyoming. The site elevation is 8,100 feet. Hosts are provided with a campsite with full hookups (electric, water, and sewer). We also maintain Cottonwood Campground on Green Mountain, 10 miles southeast of Jeffrey City. This site elevation is 7,700 feet. A host site with no hookups is provided.

We have two positions available for Campground Hosts. Both positions will receive partial uniform, the described host site and reimbursements for food and mileage as funding allows.

Fort Laramie National Historic Site

Agency: National Park Service
Season: Primarily summer
Contact: Rex Norman
HC 72 Box 389
Fort Laramie, WY 82212
Phone: (307) 837–2221

Description/Positions Available: This site is a restored military post that stands today as a reminder of America's westward expansion during the nineteenth century.

Living History Interpreters are needed to portray historical characters during the summer program. Curatorial Aides are needed to perform collection cataloging and maintenance. Maintenance Assistants will assist with building maintenance and the preservation and upkeep of park grounds.

Fossil Butte National Monument

Agency: National Park Service
Season: Summer
Contact: Marcia Fagnant
P.O. Box 592
Kemmerer, WY 83101
Phone: (307) 877–4455

Description/Positions Available: This park features the most noteworthy record of freshwater fossil fish ever found in the United States.

Volunteers are needed for interpretive programs, labor-intensive Conservation Projects, and Cultural and Natural Resource-Management Projects. An academic background in Geology or Paleontology and public speaking experience are the preferred qualifications. Shared housing is provided, as is reimbursement for mileage to and from the job site. Personal transportation is required.